Python 2.7.10 Language Reference

A catalogue record for this book is available from the Hong Kong Public Libraries.

Published in Hong Kong by Samurai Media Limited.

Email: info@samuraimedia.org

ISBN 978-988-8381-01-2

1 Introduction   **3**
    1.1   Alternate Implementations   3
    1.2   Notation   4

2 Lexical analysis   **5**
    2.1   Line structure   5
    2.2   Other tokens   8
    2.3   Identifiers and keywords   8
    2.4   Literals   9
    2.5   Operators   12
    2.6   Delimiters   13

3 Data model   **15**
    3.1   Objects, values and types   15
    3.2   The standard type hierarchy   16
    3.3   New-style and classic classes   24
    3.4   Special method names   24

4 Execution model   **41**
    4.1   Naming and binding   41
    4.2   Exceptions   43

5 Expressions   **45**
    5.1   Arithmetic conversions   45
    5.2   Atoms   45
    5.3   Primaries   50
    5.4   The power operator   54
    5.5   Unary arithmetic and bitwise operations   54
    5.6   Binary arithmetic operations   54
    5.7   Shifting operations   55
    5.8   Binary bitwise operations   56
    5.9   Comparisons   56
    5.10   Boolean operations   58
    5.11   Conditional Expressions   58
    5.12   Lambdas   58
    5.13   Expression lists   59
    5.14   Evaluation order   59
    5.15   Operator precedence   59

6 Simple statements   **61**
    6.1   Expression statements   61

6.2	Assignment statements	61
6.3	The `assert` statement	64
6.4	The `pass` statement	64
6.5	The `del` statement	64
6.6	The `print` statement	65
6.7	The `return` statement	65
6.8	The `yield` statement	66
6.9	The `raise` statement	66
6.10	The `break` statement	67
6.11	The `continue` statement	67
6.12	The `import` statement	67
6.13	The `global` statement	70
6.14	The `exec` statement	71

7 Compound statements — **73**

7.1	The `if` statement	74
7.2	The `while` statement	74
7.3	The `for` statement	74
7.4	The `try` statement	75
7.5	The `with` statement	76
7.6	Function definitions	77
7.7	Class definitions	79

8 Top-level components — **81**

8.1	Complete Python programs	81
8.2	File input	81
8.3	Interactive input	82
8.4	Expression input	82

9 Full Grammar specification — **83**

A Glossary — **87**

B About these documents — **95**

| B.1 | Contributors to the Python Documentation | 95 |

C History and License — **97**

C.1	History of the software	97
C.2	Terms and conditions for accessing or otherwise using Python	97
C.3	Licenses and Acknowledgements for Incorporated Software	100

D Copyright — **113**

Index — **115**

This reference manual describes the syntax and "core semantics" of the language. It is terse, but attempts to be exact and complete. The semantics of non-essential built-in object types and of the built-in functions and modules are described in *library-index*. For an informal introduction to the language, see *tutorial-index*. For C or C++ programmers, two additional manuals exist: *extending-index* describes the high-level picture of how to write a Python extension module, and the *c-api-index* describes the interfaces available to C/C++ programmers in detail.

CONTENTS

INTRODUCTION

This reference manual describes the Python programming language. It is not intended as a tutorial.

While I am trying to be as precise as possible, I chose to use English rather than formal specifications for everything except syntax and lexical analysis. This should make the document more understandable to the average reader, but will leave room for ambiguities. Consequently, if you were coming from Mars and tried to re-implement Python from this document alone, you might have to guess things and in fact you would probably end up implementing quite a different language. On the other hand, if you are using Python and wonder what the precise rules about a particular area of the language are, you should definitely be able to find them here. If you would like to see a more formal definition of the language, maybe you could volunteer your time — or invent a cloning machine :-).

It is dangerous to add too many implementation details to a language reference document — the implementation may change, and other implementations of the same language may work differently. On the other hand, there is currently only one Python implementation in widespread use (although alternate implementations exist), and its particular quirks are sometimes worth being mentioned, especially where the implementation imposes additional limitations. Therefore, you'll find short "implementation notes" sprinkled throughout the text.

Every Python implementation comes with a number of built-in and standard modules. These are documented in *library-index*. A few built-in modules are mentioned when they interact in a significant way with the language definition.

1.1 Alternate Implementations

Though there is one Python implementation which is by far the most popular, there are some alternate implementations which are of particular interest to different audiences.

Known implementations include:

CPython This is the original and most-maintained implementation of Python, written in C. New language features generally appear here first.

Jython Python implemented in Java. This implementation can be used as a scripting language for Java applications, or can be used to create applications using the Java class libraries. It is also often used to create tests for Java libraries. More information can be found at the Jython website.

Python for .NET This implementation actually uses the CPython implementation, but is a managed .NET application and makes .NET libraries available. It was created by Brian Lloyd. For more information, see the Python for .NET home page.

IronPython An alternate Python for .NET. Unlike Python.NET, this is a complete Python implementation that generates IL, and compiles Python code directly to .NET assemblies. It was created by Jim Hugunin, the original creator of Jython. For more information, see the IronPython website.

PyPy An implementation of Python written completely in Python. It supports several advanced features not found in other implementations like stackless support and a Just in Time compiler. One of the goals of the project is to encourage experimentation with the language itself by making it easier to modify the interpreter (since it is written in Python). Additional information is available on the PyPy project's home page.

Each of these implementations varies in some way from the language as documented in this manual, or introduces specific information beyond what's covered in the standard Python documentation. Please refer to the implementation-specific documentation to determine what else you need to know about the specific implementation you're using.

1.2 Notation

The descriptions of lexical analysis and syntax use a modified BNF grammar notation. This uses the following style of definition:

```
name        ::=   lc_letter (lc_letter | "_")*
lc_letter   ::=   "a"..."z"
```

The first line says that a `name` is an `lc_letter` followed by a sequence of zero or more `lc_letter`s and underscores. An `lc_letter` in turn is any of the single characters `'a'` through `'z'`. (This rule is actually adhered to for the names defined in lexical and grammar rules in this document.)

Each rule begins with a name (which is the name defined by the rule) and `::=`. A vertical bar (`|`) is used to separate alternatives; it is the least binding operator in this notation. A star (`*`) means zero or more repetitions of the preceding item; likewise, a plus (`+`) means one or more repetitions, and a phrase enclosed in square brackets (`[ ]`) means zero or one occurrences (in other words, the enclosed phrase is optional). The `*` and `+` operators bind as tightly as possible; parentheses are used for grouping. Literal strings are enclosed in quotes. White space is only meaningful to separate tokens. Rules are normally contained on a single line; rules with many alternatives may be formatted alternatively with each line after the first beginning with a vertical bar.

In lexical definitions (as the example above), two more conventions are used: Two literal characters separated by three dots mean a choice of any single character in the given (inclusive) range of ASCII characters. A phrase between angular brackets (`<...>`) gives an informal description of the symbol defined; e.g., this could be used to describe the notion of 'control character' if needed.

Even though the notation used is almost the same, there is a big difference between the meaning of lexical and syntactic definitions: a lexical definition operates on the individual characters of the input source, while a syntax definition operates on the stream of tokens generated by the lexical analysis. All uses of BNF in the next chapter ("Lexical Analysis") are lexical definitions; uses in subsequent chapters are syntactic definitions.

LEXICAL ANALYSIS

A Python program is read by a *parser*. Input to the parser is a stream of *tokens*, generated by the *lexical analyzer*. This chapter describes how the lexical analyzer breaks a file into tokens.

Python uses the 7-bit ASCII character set for program text.

New in version 2.3: An encoding declaration can be used to indicate that string literals and comments use an encoding different from ASCII.

For compatibility with older versions, Python only warns if it finds 8-bit characters; those warnings should be corrected by either declaring an explicit encoding, or using escape sequences if those bytes are binary data, instead of characters.

The run-time character set depends on the I/O devices connected to the program but is generally a superset of ASCII.

Future compatibility note: It may be tempting to assume that the character set for 8-bit characters is ISO Latin-1 (an ASCII superset that covers most western languages that use the Latin alphabet), but it is possible that in the future Unicode text editors will become common. These generally use the UTF-8 encoding, which is also an ASCII superset, but with very different use for the characters with ordinals 128-255. While there is no consensus on this subject yet, it is unwise to assume either Latin-1 or UTF-8, even though the current implementation appears to favor Latin-1. This applies both to the source character set and the run-time character set.

2.1 Line structure

A Python program is divided into a number of *logical lines*.

2.1.1 Logical lines

The end of a logical line is represented by the token NEWLINE. Statements cannot cross logical line boundaries except where NEWLINE is allowed by the syntax (e.g., between statements in compound statements). A logical line is constructed from one or more *physical lines* by following the explicit or implicit *line joining* rules.

2.1.2 Physical lines

A physical line is a sequence of characters terminated by an end-of-line sequence. In source files, any of the standard platform line termination sequences can be used - the Unix form using ASCII LF (linefeed), the Windows form using the ASCII sequence CR LF (return followed by linefeed), or the old Macintosh form using the ASCII CR (return) character. All of these forms can be used equally, regardless of platform.

When embedding Python, source code strings should be passed to Python APIs using the standard C conventions for newline characters (the \n character, representing ASCII LF, is the line terminator).

2.1.3 Comments

A comment starts with a hash character (#) that is not part of a string literal, and ends at the end of the physical line. A comment signifies the end of the logical line unless the implicit line joining rules are invoked. Comments are ignored by the syntax; they are not tokens.

2.1.4 Encoding declarations

If a comment in the first or second line of the Python script matches the regular expression `coding[=:]\s*([-\w.]+)`, this comment is processed as an encoding declaration; the first group of this expression names the encoding of the source code file. The encoding declaration must appear on a line of its own. If it is the second line, the first line must also be a comment-only line. The recommended forms of an encoding expression are

```
# -*- coding: <encoding-name> -*-
```

which is recognized also by GNU Emacs, and

```
# vim:fileencoding=<encoding-name>
```

which is recognized by Bram Moolenaar's VIM. In addition, if the first bytes of the file are the UTF-8 byte-order mark (`'\xef\xbb\xbf'`), the declared file encoding is UTF-8 (this is supported, among others, by Microsoft's **notepad**).

If an encoding is declared, the encoding name must be recognized by Python. The encoding is used for all lexical analysis, in particular to find the end of a string, and to interpret the contents of Unicode literals. String literals are converted to Unicode for syntactical analysis, then converted back to their original encoding before interpretation starts.

2.1.5 Explicit line joining

Two or more physical lines may be joined into logical lines using backslash characters (\), as follows: when a physical line ends in a backslash that is not part of a string literal or comment, it is joined with the following forming a single logical line, deleting the backslash and the following end-of-line character. For example:

```
if 1900 < year < 2100 and 1 <= month <= 12 \
   and 1 <= day <= 31 and 0 <= hour < 24 \
   and 0 <= minute < 60 and 0 <= second < 60:   # Looks like a valid date
       return 1
```

A line ending in a backslash cannot carry a comment. A backslash does not continue a comment. A backslash does not continue a token except for string literals (i.e., tokens other than string literals cannot be split across physical lines using a backslash). A backslash is illegal elsewhere on a line outside a string literal.

2.1.6 Implicit line joining

Expressions in parentheses, square brackets or curly braces can be split over more than one physical line without using backslashes. For example:

```
month_names = ['Januari', 'Februari', 'Maart',     # These are the
               'April',   'Mei',      'Juni',       # Dutch names
               'Juli',    'Augustus', 'September',  # for the months
               'Oktober', 'November', 'December']   # of the year
```

Implicitly continued lines can carry comments. The indentation of the continuation lines is not important. Blank continuation lines are allowed. There is no NEWLINE token between implicit continuation lines. Implicitly continued lines can also occur within triple-quoted strings (see below); in that case they cannot carry comments.

2.1.7 Blank lines

A logical line that contains only spaces, tabs, formfeeds and possibly a comment, is ignored (i.e., no NEWLINE token is generated). During interactive input of statements, handling of a blank line may differ depending on the implementation of the read-eval-print loop. In the standard implementation, an entirely blank logical line (i.e. one containing not even whitespace or a comment) terminates a multi-line statement.

2.1.8 Indentation

Leading whitespace (spaces and tabs) at the beginning of a logical line is used to compute the indentation level of the line, which in turn is used to determine the grouping of statements.

First, tabs are replaced (from left to right) by one to eight spaces such that the total number of characters up to and including the replacement is a multiple of eight (this is intended to be the same rule as used by Unix). The total number of spaces preceding the first non-blank character then determines the line's indentation. Indentation cannot be split over multiple physical lines using backslashes; the whitespace up to the first backslash determines the indentation.

Cross-platform compatibility note: because of the nature of text editors on non-UNIX platforms, it is unwise to use a mixture of spaces and tabs for the indentation in a single source file. It should also be noted that different platforms may explicitly limit the maximum indentation level.

A formfeed character may be present at the start of the line; it will be ignored for the indentation calculations above. Formfeed characters occurring elsewhere in the leading whitespace have an undefined effect (for instance, they may reset the space count to zero).

The indentation levels of consecutive lines are used to generate INDENT and DEDENT tokens, using a stack, as follows.

Before the first line of the file is read, a single zero is pushed on the stack; this will never be popped off again. The numbers pushed on the stack will always be strictly increasing from bottom to top. At the beginning of each logical line, the line's indentation level is compared to the top of the stack. If it is equal, nothing happens. If it is larger, it is pushed on the stack, and one INDENT token is generated. If it is smaller, it *must* be one of the numbers occurring on the stack; all numbers on the stack that are larger are popped off, and for each number popped off a DEDENT token is generated. At the end of the file, a DEDENT token is generated for each number remaining on the stack that is larger than zero.

Here is an example of a correctly (though confusingly) indented piece of Python code:

```python
def perm(l):
                # Compute the list of all permutations of l
    if len(l) <= 1:
                    return [l]
    r = []
    for i in range(len(l)):
            s = l[:i] + l[i+1:]
            p = perm(s)
            for x in p:
              r.append(l[i:i+1] + x)
    return r
```

The following example shows various indentation errors:

```python
 def perm(l):                   # error: first line indented
for i in range(len(l)):         # error: not indented
    s = l[:i] + l[i+1:]
        p = perm(l[:i] + l[i+1:])   # error: unexpected indent
        for x in p:
```

```
            r.append(l[i:i+1] + x)
      return r                    # error: inconsistent dedent
```

(Actually, the first three errors are detected by the parser; only the last error is found by the lexical analyzer — the indentation of `return r` does not match a level popped off the stack.)

2.1.9 Whitespace between tokens

Except at the beginning of a logical line or in string literals, the whitespace characters space, tab and formfeed can be used interchangeably to separate tokens. Whitespace is needed between two tokens only if their concatenation could otherwise be interpreted as a different token (e.g., ab is one token, but a b is two tokens).

2.2 Other tokens

Besides NEWLINE, INDENT and DEDENT, the following categories of tokens exist: *identifiers*, *keywords*, *literals*, *operators*, and *delimiters*. Whitespace characters (other than line terminators, discussed earlier) are not tokens, but serve to delimit tokens. Where ambiguity exists, a token comprises the longest possible string that forms a legal token, when read from left to right.

2.3 Identifiers and keywords

Identifiers (also referred to as *names*) are described by the following lexical definitions:

```
identifier  ::=   (letter|"_") (letter | digit | "_")*
letter      ::=   lowercase | uppercase
lowercase   ::=   "a"..."z"
uppercase   ::=   "A"..."Z"
digit       ::=   "0"..."9"
```

Identifiers are unlimited in length. Case is significant.

2.3.1 Keywords

The following identifiers are used as reserved words, or *keywords* of the language, and cannot be used as ordinary identifiers. They must be spelled exactly as written here:

```
and         del         from        not         while
as          elif        global      or          with
assert      else        if          pass        yield
break       except      import      print
class       exec        in          raise
continue    finally     is          return
def         for         lambda      try
```

Changed in version 2.4: None became a constant and is now recognized by the compiler as a name for the built-in object None. Although it is not a keyword, you cannot assign a different object to it.

Changed in version 2.5: Using `as` and `with` as identifiers triggers a warning. To use them as keywords, enable the `with_statement` future feature .

Changed in version 2.6: `as` and `with` are full keywords.

2.3.2 Reserved classes of identifiers

Certain classes of identifiers (besides keywords) have special meanings. These classes are identified by the patterns of leading and trailing underscore characters:

`_*` Not imported by `from module import *`. The special identifier _ is used in the interactive interpreter to store the result of the last evaluation; it is stored in the `__builtin__` module. When not in interactive mode, _ has no special meaning and is not defined. See section *The import statement*.

> **Note:** The name _ is often used in conjunction with internationalization; refer to the documentation for the `gettext` module for more information on this convention.

`__*__` System-defined names. These names are defined by the interpreter and its implementation (including the standard library). Current system names are discussed in the *Special method names* section and elsewhere. More will likely be defined in future versions of Python. *Any* use of `__*__` names, in any context, that does not follow explicitly documented use, is subject to breakage without warning.

`__*` Class-private names. Names in this category, when used within the context of a class definition, are re-written to use a mangled form to help avoid name clashes between "private" attributes of base and derived classes. See section *Identifiers (Names)*.

2.4 Literals

Literals are notations for constant values of some built-in types.

2.4.1 String literals

String literals are described by the following lexical definitions:

```
stringliteral      ::=   [stringprefix](shortstring | longstring)
stringprefix       ::=   "r" | "u" | "ur" | "R" | "U" | "UR" | "Ur" | "uR"
                         | "b" | "B" | "br" | "Br" | "bR" | "BR"
shortstring        ::=   "'" shortstringitem* "'" | '"' shortstringitem* '"'
longstring         ::=   "'''" longstringitem* "'''"
                         | '"""' longstringitem* '"""'
shortstringitem    ::=   shortstringchar | escapeseq
longstringitem     ::=   longstringchar | escapeseq
shortstringchar    ::=   <any source character except "\" or newline or the quote>
longstringchar     ::=   <any source character except "\">
escapeseq          ::=   "\" <any ASCII character>
```

One syntactic restriction not indicated by these productions is that whitespace is not allowed between the `stringprefix` and the rest of the string literal. The source character set is defined by the encoding declaration; it is ASCII if no encoding declaration is given in the source file; see section *Encoding declarations*.

In plain English: String literals can be enclosed in matching single quotes (') or double quotes ("). They can also be enclosed in matching groups of three single or double quotes (these are generally referred to as *triple-quoted strings*). The backslash (\) character is used to escape characters that otherwise have a special meaning, such as newline, backslash itself, or the quote character. String literals may optionally be prefixed with a letter 'r' or 'R'; such strings are called *raw strings* and use different rules for interpreting backslash escape sequences. A prefix of ′u′ or ′U′ makes the string a Unicode string. Unicode strings use the Unicode character set as defined by the Unicode Consortium and ISO 10646. Some additional escape sequences, described below, are available in Unicode strings. A prefix of ′b′ or ′B′ is ignored in Python 2; it indicates that the literal should become a bytes literal in Python 3 (e.g. when code is automatically converted with 2to3). A ′u′ or ′b′ prefix may be followed by an ′r′ prefix.

In triple-quoted strings, unescaped newlines and quotes are allowed (and are retained), except that three unescaped quotes in a row terminate the string. (A "quote" is the character used to open the string, i.e. either ′ or ".)

Unless an ′r′ or ′R′ prefix is present, escape sequences in strings are interpreted according to rules similar to those used by Standard C. The recognized escape sequences are:

Escape Sequence	Meaning	Notes
\newline	Ignored	
\\	Backslash (\)	
\'	Single quote (′)	
\"	Double quote (")	
\a	ASCII Bell (BEL)	
\b	ASCII Backspace (BS)	
\f	ASCII Formfeed (FF)	
\n	ASCII Linefeed (LF)	
\N{name}	Character named *name* in the Unicode database (Unicode only)	
\r	ASCII Carriage Return (CR)	
\t	ASCII Horizontal Tab (TAB)	
\uxxxx	Character with 16-bit hex value *xxxx* (Unicode only)	(1)
\Uxxxxxxxx	Character with 32-bit hex value *xxxxxxxx* (Unicode only)	(2)
\v	ASCII Vertical Tab (VT)	
\ooo	Character with octal value *ooo*	(3,5)
\xhh	Character with hex value *hh*	(4,5)

Notes:

1. Individual code units which form parts of a surrogate pair can be encoded using this escape sequence.

2. Any Unicode character can be encoded this way, but characters outside the Basic Multilingual Plane (BMP) will be encoded using a surrogate pair if Python is compiled to use 16-bit code units (the default).

3. As in Standard C, up to three octal digits are accepted.

4. Unlike in Standard C, exactly two hex digits are required.

5. In a string literal, hexadecimal and octal escapes denote the byte with the given value; it is not necessary that the byte encodes a character in the source character set. In a Unicode literal, these escapes denote a Unicode character with the given value.

Unlike Standard C, all unrecognized escape sequences are left in the string unchanged, i.e., *the backslash is left in the string*. (This behavior is useful when debugging: if an escape sequence is mistyped, the resulting output is more easily recognized as broken.) It is also important to note that the escape sequences marked as "(Unicode only)" in the table above fall into the category of unrecognized escapes for non-Unicode string literals.

When an ′r′ or ′R′ prefix is present, a character following a backslash is included in the string without change, and *all backslashes are left in the string*. For example, the string literal r"\n" consists of two characters: a backslash and a lowercase ′n′. String quotes can be escaped with a backslash, but the backslash remains in the string; for example, r"\"" is a valid string literal consisting of two characters: a backslash and a double quote; r"\" is not a valid string literal (even a raw string cannot end in an odd number of backslashes). Specifically, *a raw string cannot end in a single backslash* (since the backslash would escape the following quote character). Note also that a single backslash followed by a newline is interpreted as those two characters as part of the string, *not* as a line continuation.

When an ′r′ or ′R′ prefix is used in conjunction with a ′u′ or ′U′ prefix, then the \uXXXX and \UXXXXXXXX escape sequences are processed while *all other backslashes are left in the string*. For example, the string literal ur"\u0062\n" consists of three Unicode characters: 'LATIN SMALL LETTER B', 'REVERSE SOLIDUS', and 'LATIN SMALL LETTER N'. Backslashes can be escaped with a preceding backslash; however, both remain in the string. As a result, \uXXXX escape sequences are only recognized when there are an odd number of backslashes.

2.4.2 String literal concatenation

Multiple adjacent string literals (delimited by whitespace), possibly using different quoting conventions, are allowed, and their meaning is the same as their concatenation. Thus, "hello" 'world' is equivalent to "helloworld". This feature can be used to reduce the number of backslashes needed, to split long strings conveniently across long lines, or even to add comments to parts of strings, for example:

```
re.compile("[A-Za-z_]"       # letter or underscore
           "[A-Za-z0-9_]*"    # letter, digit or underscore
          )
```

Note that this feature is defined at the syntactical level, but implemented at compile time. The '+' operator must be used to concatenate string expressions at run time. Also note that literal concatenation can use different quoting styles for each component (even mixing raw strings and triple quoted strings).

2.4.3 Numeric literals

There are four types of numeric literals: plain integers, long integers, floating point numbers, and imaginary numbers. There are no complex literals (complex numbers can be formed by adding a real number and an imaginary number).

Note that numeric literals do not include a sign; a phrase like -1 is actually an expression composed of the unary operator '-' and the literal 1.

2.4.4 Integer and long integer literals

Integer and long integer literals are described by the following lexical definitions:

```
longinteger    ::=   integer ("l" | "L")
integer        ::=   decimalinteger | octinteger | hexinteger | bininteger
decimalinteger ::=   nonzerodigit digit* | "0"
octinteger     ::=   "0" ("o" | "O") octdigit+ | "0" octdigit+
hexinteger     ::=   "0" ("x" | "X") hexdigit+
bininteger     ::=   "0" ("b" | "B") bindigit+
nonzerodigit   ::=   "1"..."9"
octdigit       ::=   "0"..."7"
bindigit       ::=   "0" | "1"
hexdigit       ::=   digit | "a"..."f" | "A"..."F"
```

Although both lower case 'l' and upper case 'L' are allowed as suffix for long integers, it is strongly recommended to always use 'L', since the letter 'l' looks too much like the digit '1'.

Plain integer literals that are above the largest representable plain integer (e.g., 2147483647 when using 32-bit arithmetic) are accepted as if they were long integers instead. [1] There is no limit for long integer literals apart from what can be stored in available memory.

Some examples of plain integer literals (first row) and long integer literals (second and third rows):

---

[1] In versions of Python prior to 2.4, octal and hexadecimal literals in the range just above the largest representable plain integer but below the largest unsigned 32-bit number (on a machine using 32-bit arithmetic), 4294967296, were taken as the negative plain integer obtained by subtracting 4294967296 from their unsigned value.

```
7       2147483647                              0177
3L      79228162514264337593543950336L         0377L    0x100000000L
        79228162514264337593543950336                   0xdeadbeef
```

2.4.5 Floating point literals

Floating point literals are described by the following lexical definitions:

```
floatnumber      ::=    pointfloat | exponentfloat
pointfloat       ::=    [intpart] fraction | intpart "."
exponentfloat    ::=    (intpart | pointfloat) exponent
intpart          ::=    digit+
fraction         ::=    "." digit+
exponent         ::=    ("e" | "E") ["+" | "-"] digit+
```

Note that the integer and exponent parts of floating point numbers can look like octal integers, but are interpreted using radix 10. For example, `077e010` is legal, and denotes the same number as `77e10`. The allowed range of floating point literals is implementation-dependent. Some examples of floating point literals:

```
3.14    10.    .001    1e100    3.14e-10    0e0
```

Note that numeric literals do not include a sign; a phrase like `-1` is actually an expression composed of the unary operator `-` and the literal `1`.

2.4.6 Imaginary literals

Imaginary literals are described by the following lexical definitions:

```
imagnumber   ::=    (floatnumber | intpart) ("j" | "J")
```

An imaginary literal yields a complex number with a real part of 0.0. Complex numbers are represented as a pair of floating point numbers and have the same restrictions on their range. To create a complex number with a nonzero real part, add a floating point number to it, e.g., `(3+4j)`. Some examples of imaginary literals:

```
3.14j    10.j    10j    .001j    1e100j    3.14e-10j
```

2.5 Operators

The following tokens are operators:

```
+       -       *       **      /       //      %
<<      >>      &       |       ^       ~
<       >       <=      >=      ==      !=      <>
```

The comparison operators `<>` and `!=` are alternate spellings of the same operator. `!=` is the preferred spelling; `<>` is obsolescent.

2.6 Delimiters

The following tokens serve as delimiters in the grammar:

(	)	[	]	{	}	@
,	:	.	`	=	;	
+=	-=	*=	/=	//=	%=	
&=	|=	^=	>>=	<<=	**=	

The period can also occur in floating-point and imaginary literals. A sequence of three periods has a special meaning as an ellipsis in slices. The second half of the list, the augmented assignment operators, serve lexically as delimiters, but also perform an operation.

The following printing ASCII characters have special meaning as part of other tokens or are otherwise significant to the lexical analyzer:

'	"	#	\

The following printing ASCII characters are not used in Python. Their occurrence outside string literals and comments is an unconditional error:

$	?

DATA MODEL

3.1 Objects, values and types

Objects are Python's abstraction for data. All data in a Python program is represented by objects or by relations between objects. (In a sense, and in conformance to Von Neumann's model of a "stored program computer," code is also represented by objects.)

Every object has an identity, a type and a value. An object's *identity* never changes once it has been created; you may think of it as the object's address in memory. The '`is`' operator compares the identity of two objects; the `id()` function returns an integer representing its identity (currently implemented as its address). An object's *type* is also unchangeable. [1] An object's type determines the operations that the object supports (e.g., "does it have a length?") and also defines the possible values for objects of that type. The `type()` function returns an object's type (which is an object itself). The *value* of some objects can change. Objects whose value can change are said to be *mutable*; objects whose value is unchangeable once they are created are called *immutable*. (The value of an immutable container object that contains a reference to a mutable object can change when the latter's value is changed; however the container is still considered immutable, because the collection of objects it contains cannot be changed. So, immutability is not strictly the same as having an unchangeable value, it is more subtle.) An object's mutability is determined by its type; for instance, numbers, strings and tuples are immutable, while dictionaries and lists are mutable.

Objects are never explicitly destroyed; however, when they become unreachable they may be garbage-collected. An implementation is allowed to postpone garbage collection or omit it altogether — it is a matter of implementation quality how garbage collection is implemented, as long as no objects are collected that are still reachable.

CPython implementation detail: CPython currently uses a reference-counting scheme with (optional) delayed detection of cyclically linked garbage, which collects most objects as soon as they become unreachable, but is not guaranteed to collect garbage containing circular references. See the documentation of the `gc` module for information on controlling the collection of cyclic garbage. Other implementations act differently and CPython may change. Do not depend on immediate finalization of objects when they become unreachable (ex: always close files).

Note that the use of the implementation's tracing or debugging facilities may keep objects alive that would normally be collectable. Also note that catching an exception with a '`try...except`' statement may keep objects alive.

Some objects contain references to "external" resources such as open files or windows. It is understood that these resources are freed when the object is garbage-collected, but since garbage collection is not guaranteed to happen, such objects also provide an explicit way to release the external resource, usually a `close()` method. Programs are strongly recommended to explicitly close such objects. The '`try...finally`' statement provides a convenient way to do this.

Some objects contain references to other objects; these are called *containers*. Examples of containers are tuples, lists and dictionaries. The references are part of a container's value. In most cases, when we talk about the value of a container, we imply the values, not the identities of the contained objects; however, when we talk about the mutability

---

[1] It *is* possible in some cases to change an object's type, under certain controlled conditions. It generally isn't a good idea though, since it can lead to some very strange behaviour if it is handled incorrectly.

of a container, only the identities of the immediately contained objects are implied. So, if an immutable container (like a tuple) contains a reference to a mutable object, its value changes if that mutable object is changed.

Types affect almost all aspects of object behavior. Even the importance of object identity is affected in some sense: for immutable types, operations that compute new values may actually return a reference to any existing object with the same type and value, while for mutable objects this is not allowed. E.g., after a = 1; b = 1, a and b may or may not refer to the same object with the value one, depending on the implementation, but after c = []; d = [], c and d are guaranteed to refer to two different, unique, newly created empty lists. (Note that c = d = [] assigns the same object to both c and d.)

3.2 The standard type hierarchy

Below is a list of the types that are built into Python. Extension modules (written in C, Java, or other languages, depending on the implementation) can define additional types. Future versions of Python may add types to the type hierarchy (e.g., rational numbers, efficiently stored arrays of integers, etc.).

Some of the type descriptions below contain a paragraph listing 'special attributes.' These are attributes that provide access to the implementation and are not intended for general use. Their definition may change in the future.

None This type has a single value. There is a single object with this value. This object is accessed through the built-in name None. It is used to signify the absence of a value in many situations, e.g., it is returned from functions that don't explicitly return anything. Its truth value is false.

NotImplemented This type has a single value. There is a single object with this value. This object is accessed through the built-in name NotImplemented. Numeric methods and rich comparison methods may return this value if they do not implement the operation for the operands provided. (The interpreter will then try the reflected operation, or some other fallback, depending on the operator.) Its truth value is true.

Ellipsis This type has a single value. There is a single object with this value. This object is accessed through the built-in name Ellipsis. It is used to indicate the presence of the ... syntax in a slice. Its truth value is true.

numbers.Number These are created by numeric literals and returned as results by arithmetic operators and arithmetic built-in functions. Numeric objects are immutable; once created their value never changes. Python numbers are of course strongly related to mathematical numbers, but subject to the limitations of numerical representation in computers.

Python distinguishes between integers, floating point numbers, and complex numbers:

numbers.Integral These represent elements from the mathematical set of integers (positive and negative).

There are three types of integers:

Plain integers These represent numbers in the range -2147483648 through 2147483647. (The range may be larger on machines with a larger natural word size, but not smaller.) When the result of an operation would fall outside this range, the result is normally returned as a long integer (in some cases, the exception OverflowError is raised instead). For the purpose of shift and mask operations, integers are assumed to have a binary, 2's complement notation using 32 or more bits, and hiding no bits from the user (i.e., all 4294967296 different bit patterns correspond to different values).

Long integers These represent numbers in an unlimited range, subject to available (virtual) memory only. For the purpose of shift and mask operations, a binary representation is assumed, and negative numbers are represented in a variant of 2's complement which gives the illusion of an infinite string of sign bits extending to the left.

Booleans These represent the truth values False and True. The two objects representing the values False and True are the only Boolean objects. The Boolean type is a subtype of plain integers, and Boolean values behave like the values 0 and 1, respectively, in almost all contexts, the exception being that when converted to a string, the strings "False" or "True" are returned, respectively.

The rules for integer representation are intended to give the most meaningful interpretation of shift and mask operations involving negative integers and the least surprises when switching between the plain and long integer domains. Any operation, if it yields a result in the plain integer domain, will yield the same result in the long integer domain or when using mixed operands. The switch between domains is transparent to the programmer.

numbers.Real (float) These represent machine-level double precision floating point numbers. You are at the mercy of the underlying machine architecture (and C or Java implementation) for the accepted range and handling of overflow. Python does not support single-precision floating point numbers; the savings in processor and memory usage that are usually the reason for using these are dwarfed by the overhead of using objects in Python, so there is no reason to complicate the language with two kinds of floating point numbers.

numbers.Complex These represent complex numbers as a pair of machine-level double precision floating point numbers. The same caveats apply as for floating point numbers. The real and imaginary parts of a complex number z can be retrieved through the read-only attributes z.real and z.imag.

Sequences These represent finite ordered sets indexed by non-negative numbers. The built-in function `len()` returns the number of items of a sequence. When the length of a sequence is n, the index set contains the numbers 0, 1, ..., n-1. Item i of sequence a is selected by `a[i]`.

Sequences also support slicing: `a[i:j]` selects all items with index k such that $i <= k < j$. When used as an expression, a slice is a sequence of the same type. This implies that the index set is renumbered so that it starts at 0.

Some sequences also support "extended slicing" with a third "step" parameter: `a[i:j:k]` selects all items of a with index x where $x = i + n*k$, $n >= 0$ and $i <= x < j$.

Sequences are distinguished according to their mutability:

Immutable sequences An object of an immutable sequence type cannot change once it is created. (If the object contains references to other objects, these other objects may be mutable and may be changed; however, the collection of objects directly referenced by an immutable object cannot change.)

The following types are immutable sequences:

Strings The items of a string are characters. There is no separate character type; a character is represented by a string of one item. Characters represent (at least) 8-bit bytes. The built-in functions `chr()` and `ord()` convert between characters and nonnegative integers representing the byte values. Bytes with the values 0-127 usually represent the corresponding ASCII values, but the interpretation of values is up to the program. The string data type is also used to represent arrays of bytes, e.g., to hold data read from a file.

(On systems whose native character set is not ASCII, strings may use EBCDIC in their internal representation, provided the functions `chr()` and `ord()` implement a mapping between ASCII and EBCDIC, and string comparison preserves the ASCII order. Or perhaps someone can propose a better rule?)

Unicode The items of a Unicode object are Unicode code units. A Unicode code unit is represented by a Unicode object of one item and can hold either a 16-bit or 32-bit value representing a Unicode ordinal (the maximum value for the ordinal is given in `sys.maxunicode`, and depends on how Python is configured at compile time). Surrogate pairs may be present in the Unicode object, and will be reported as two separate items. The built-in functions `unichr()` and `ord()` convert between code units and nonnegative integers representing the Unicode ordinals as defined in the Unicode Standard 3.0. Conversion from and to other encodings are possible through the Unicode method `encode()` and the built-in function `unicode()`.

Tuples The items of a tuple are arbitrary Python objects. Tuples of two or more items are formed by comma-separated lists of expressions. A tuple of one item (a 'singleton') can be formed by affixing a comma to an expression (an expression by itself does not create a tuple, since parentheses must be usable for grouping of expressions). An empty tuple can be formed by an empty pair of parentheses.

Mutable sequences Mutable sequences can be changed after they are created. The subscription and slicing notations can be used as the target of assignment and `del` (delete) statements.

There are currently two intrinsic mutable sequence types:

Lists The items of a list are arbitrary Python objects. Lists are formed by placing a comma-separated list of expressions in square brackets. (Note that there are no special cases needed to form lists of length 0 or 1.)

Byte Arrays A bytearray object is a mutable array. They are created by the built-in `bytearray()` constructor. Aside from being mutable (and hence unhashable), byte arrays otherwise provide the same interface and functionality as immutable bytes objects.

The extension module `array` provides an additional example of a mutable sequence type.

Set types These represent unordered, finite sets of unique, immutable objects. As such, they cannot be indexed by any subscript. However, they can be iterated over, and the built-in function `len()` returns the number of items in a set. Common uses for sets are fast membership testing, removing duplicates from a sequence, and computing mathematical operations such as intersection, union, difference, and symmetric difference.

For set elements, the same immutability rules apply as for dictionary keys. Note that numeric types obey the normal rules for numeric comparison: if two numbers compare equal (e.g., `1` and `1.0`), only one of them can be contained in a set.

There are currently two intrinsic set types:

Sets These represent a mutable set. They are created by the built-in `set()` constructor and can be modified afterwards by several methods, such as `add()`.

Frozen sets These represent an immutable set. They are created by the built-in `frozenset()` constructor. As a frozenset is immutable and *hashable*, it can be used again as an element of another set, or as a dictionary key.

Mappings These represent finite sets of objects indexed by arbitrary index sets. The subscript notation `a[k]` selects the item indexed by `k` from the mapping `a`; this can be used in expressions and as the target of assignments or `del` statements. The built-in function `len()` returns the number of items in a mapping.

There is currently a single intrinsic mapping type:

Dictionaries These represent finite sets of objects indexed by nearly arbitrary values. The only types of values not acceptable as keys are values containing lists or dictionaries or other mutable types that are compared by value rather than by object identity, the reason being that the efficient implementation of dictionaries requires a key's hash value to remain constant. Numeric types used for keys obey the normal rules for numeric comparison: if two numbers compare equal (e.g., `1` and `1.0`) then they can be used interchangeably to index the same dictionary entry.

Dictionaries are mutable; they can be created by the `{...}` notation (see section *Dictionary displays*).

The extension modules `dbm`, `gdbm`, and `bsddb` provide additional examples of mapping types.

Callable types These are the types to which the function call operation (see section *Calls*) can be applied:

User-defined functions A user-defined function object is created by a function definition (see section *Function definitions*). It should be called with an argument list containing the same number of items as the function's formal parameter list.

Special attributes:

Attribute	Meaning	
`__doc__ func_doc`	The function's documentation string, or `None` if unavailable.	Writable
`__name__ func_name`	The function's name.	Writable
`__module__`	The name of the module the function was defined in, or `None` if unavailable.	Writable
`__defaults__ func_defaults`	A tuple containing default argument values for those arguments that have defaults, or `None` if no arguments have a default value.	Writable
`__code__ func_code`	The code object representing the compiled function body.	Writable
`__globals__ func_globals`	A reference to the dictionary that holds the function's global variables — the global namespace of the module in which the function was defined.	Read-only
`__dict__ func_dict`	The namespace supporting arbitrary function attributes.	Writable
`__closure__ func_closure`	`None` or a tuple of cells that contain bindings for the function's free variables.	Read-only

Most of the attributes labelled "Writable" check the type of the assigned value.

Changed in version 2.4: `func_name` is now writable.

Changed in version 2.6: The double-underscore attributes `__closure__`, `__code__`, `__defaults__`, and `__globals__` were introduced as aliases for the corresponding `func_*` attributes for forwards compatibility with Python 3.

Function objects also support getting and setting arbitrary attributes, which can be used, for example, to attach metadata to functions. Regular attribute dot-notation is used to get and set such attributes. *Note that the current implementation only supports function attributes on user-defined functions. Function attributes on built-in functions may be supported in the future.*

Additional information about a function's definition can be retrieved from its code object; see the description of internal types below.

User-defined methods A user-defined method object combines a class, a class instance (or `None`) and any callable object (normally a user-defined function).

Special read-only attributes: `im_self` is the class instance object, `im_func` is the function object; `im_class` is the class of `im_self` for bound methods or the class that asked for the method for unbound methods; `__doc__` is the method's documentation (same as `im_func.__doc__`); `__name__` is the method name (same as `im_func.__name__`); `__module__` is the name of the module the method was defined in, or `None` if unavailable.

Changed in version 2.2: `im_self` used to refer to the class that defined the method.

Changed in version 2.6: For Python 3 forward-compatibility, `im_func` is also available as `__func__`, and `im_self` as `__self__`.

Methods also support accessing (but not setting) the arbitrary function attributes on the underlying function object.

User-defined method objects may be created when getting an attribute of a class (perhaps via an instance of that class), if that attribute is a user-defined function object, an unbound user-defined method object, or a class method object. When the attribute is a user-defined method object, a new method object is only created if the class from which it is being retrieved is the same as, or a derived class of, the class stored in the original method object; otherwise, the original method object is used as it is.

When a user-defined method object is created by retrieving a user-defined function object from a class, its `im_self` attribute is `None` and the method object is said to be unbound. When one is created by retrieving a user-defined function object from a class via one of its instances, its `im_self` attribute is the instance, and the method object is said to be bound. In either case, the new method's `im_class` attribute is the class from which the retrieval takes place, and its `im_func` attribute is the original function object.

When a user-defined method object is created by retrieving another method object from a class or instance, the behaviour is the same as for a function object, except that the `im_func` attribute of the new instance is not the original method object but its `im_func` attribute.

When a user-defined method object is created by retrieving a class method object from a class or instance, its `im_self` attribute is the class itself, and its `im_func` attribute is the function object underlying the class method.

When an unbound user-defined method object is called, the underlying function (`im_func`) is called, with the restriction that the first argument must be an instance of the proper class (`im_class`) or of a derived class thereof.

When a bound user-defined method object is called, the underlying function (`im_func`) is called, inserting the class instance (`im_self`) in front of the argument list. For instance, when `C` is a class which contains a definition for a function `f()`, and `x` is an instance of `C`, calling `x.f(1)` is equivalent to calling `C.f(x, 1)`.

When a user-defined method object is derived from a class method object, the "class instance" stored in `im_self` will actually be the class itself, so that calling either `x.f(1)` or `C.f(1)` is equivalent to calling `f(C,1)` where `f` is the underlying function.

Note that the transformation from function object to (unbound or bound) method object happens each time the attribute is retrieved from the class or instance. In some cases, a fruitful optimization is to assign the attribute to a local variable and call that local variable. Also notice that this transformation only happens for user-defined functions; other callable objects (and all non-callable objects) are retrieved without transformation. It is also important to note that user-defined functions which are attributes of a class instance are not converted to bound methods; this *only* happens when the function is an attribute of the class.

Generator functions A function or method which uses the `yield` statement (see section *The yield statement*) is called a *generator function*. Such a function, when called, always returns an iterator object which can be used to execute the body of the function: calling the iterator's `next()` method will cause the function to execute until it provides a value using the `yield` statement. When the function executes a `return` statement or falls off the end, a `StopIteration` exception is raised and the iterator will have reached the end of the set of values to be returned.

Built-in functions A built-in function object is a wrapper around a C function. Examples of built-in functions are `len()` and `math.sin()` (`math` is a standard built-in module). The number and type of the arguments are determined by the C function. Special read-only attributes: `__doc__` is the function's documentation string, or `None` if unavailable; `__name__` is the function's name; `__self__` is set to `None` (but see the next item); `__module__` is the name of the module the function was defined in or `None` if unavailable.

Built-in methods This is really a different disguise of a built-in function, this time containing an object passed to the C function as an implicit extra argument. An example of a built-in method is `alist.append()`, assuming *alist* is a list object. In this case, the special read-only attribute `__self__` is set to the object denoted by *alist*.

Class Types Class types, or "new-style classes," are callable. These objects normally act as factories for new instances of themselves, but variations are possible for class types that override `__new__()`. The arguments of the call are passed to `__new__()` and, in the typical case, to `__init__()` to initialize the new instance.

Classic Classes Class objects are described below. When a class object is called, a new class instance (also described below) is created and returned. This implies a call to the class's `__init__()` method if it has one. Any arguments are passed on to the `__init__()` method. If there is no `__init__()` method, the class must be called without arguments.

Class instances Class instances are described below. Class instances are callable only when the class has a `__call__()` method; `x(arguments)` is a shorthand for `x.__call__(arguments)`.

Modules Modules are imported by the `import` statement (see section *The import statement*). A module object has a namespace implemented by a dictionary object (this is the dictionary referenced by the func_globals attribute of functions defined in the module). Attribute references are translated to lookups in this dictionary, e.g., `m.x` is equivalent to `m.__dict__["x"]`. A module object does not contain the code object used to initialize the module (since it isn't needed once the initialization is done).

Attribute assignment updates the module's namespace dictionary, e.g., `m.x = 1` is equivalent to `m.__dict__["x"] = 1`.

Special read-only attribute: `__dict__` is the module's namespace as a dictionary object.

CPython implementation detail: Because of the way CPython clears module dictionaries, the module dictionary will be cleared when the module falls out of scope even if the dictionary still has live references. To avoid this, copy the dictionary or keep the module around while using its dictionary directly.

Predefined (writable) attributes: `__name__` is the module's name; `__doc__` is the module's documentation string, or `None` if unavailable; `__file__` is the pathname of the file from which the module was loaded, if it was loaded from a file. The `__file__` attribute is not present for C modules that are statically linked into the interpreter; for extension modules loaded dynamically from a shared library, it is the pathname of the shared library file.

Classes Both class types (new-style classes) and class objects (old-style/classic classes) are typically created by class definitions (see section *Class definitions*). A class has a namespace implemented by a dictionary object. Class attribute references are translated to lookups in this dictionary, e.g., `C.x` is translated to `C.__dict__["x"]` (although for new-style classes in particular there are a number of hooks which allow for other means of locating attributes). When the attribute name is not found there, the attribute search continues in the base classes. For old-style classes, the search is depth-first, left-to-right in the order of occurrence in the base class list. New-style classes use the more complex C3 method resolution order which behaves correctly even in the presence of 'diamond' inheritance structures where there are multiple inheritance paths leading back to a common ancestor. Additional details on the C3 MRO used by new-style classes can be found in the documentation accompanying the 2.3 release at https://www.python.org/download/releases/2.3/mro/.

When a class attribute reference (for class C, say) would yield a user-defined function object or an unbound user-defined method object whose associated class is either C or one of its base classes, it is transformed into an unbound user-defined method object whose `im_class` attribute is C. When it would yield a class method object, it is transformed into a bound user-defined method object whose `im_self` attribute is C. When it would yield a static method object, it is transformed into the object wrapped by the static method object. See section *Implementing Descriptors* for another way in which attributes retrieved from a class may differ from those actually contained in its `__dict__` (note that only new-style classes support descriptors).

Class attribute assignments update the class's dictionary, never the dictionary of a base class.

A class object can be called (see above) to yield a class instance (see below).

Special attributes: `__name__` is the class name; `__module__` is the module name in which the class was defined; `__dict__` is the dictionary containing the class's namespace; `__bases__` is a tuple (possibly empty or a singleton) containing the base classes, in the order of their occurrence in the base class list; `__doc__` is the class's documentation string, or None if undefined.

Class instances A class instance is created by calling a class object (see above). A class instance has a namespace implemented as a dictionary which is the first place in which attribute references are searched. When an attribute is not found there, and the instance's class has an attribute by that name, the search continues with the class attributes. If a class attribute is found that is a user-defined function object or an unbound user-defined method object whose associated class is the class (call it C) of the instance for which the attribute reference was initiated or one of its bases, it is transformed into a bound user-defined method object whose `im_class` attribute is C and whose `im_self` attribute is the instance. Static method and class method objects are also transformed, as if they had been retrieved from class C; see above under "Classes". See section *Implementing Descriptors* for another way in which attributes of a class retrieved via its instances may differ from the objects actually stored in the class's `__dict__`. If no class attribute is found, and the object's class has a `__getattr__`() method, that is called to satisfy the lookup.

Attribute assignments and deletions update the instance's dictionary, never a class's dictionary. If the class has a `__setattr__`() or `__delattr__`() method, this is called instead of updating the instance dictionary directly.

Class instances can pretend to be numbers, sequences, or mappings if they have methods with certain special names. See section *Special method names*.

Special attributes: `__dict__` is the attribute dictionary; `__class__` is the instance's class.

Files A file object represents an open file. File objects are created by the `open()` built-in function, and also by `os.popen()`, `os.fdopen()`, and the `makefile()` method of socket objects (and perhaps by other functions or methods provided by extension modules). The objects `sys.stdin`, `sys.stdout` and `sys.stderr` are initialized to file objects corresponding to the interpreter's standard input, output and error streams. See *bltin-file-objects* for complete documentation of file objects.

Internal types A few types used internally by the interpreter are exposed to the user. Their definitions may change with future versions of the interpreter, but they are mentioned here for completeness.

Code objects Code objects represent *byte-compiled* executable Python code, or *bytecode*. The difference between a code object and a function object is that the function object contains an explicit reference to the function's globals (the module in which it was defined), while a code object contains no context; also the default argument values are stored in the function object, not in the code object (because they represent values calculated at run-time). Unlike function objects, code objects are immutable and contain no references (directly or indirectly) to mutable objects.

Special read-only attributes: `co_name` gives the function name; `co_argcount` is the number of positional arguments (including arguments with default values); `co_nlocals` is the number of local variables used by the function (including arguments); `co_varnames` is a tuple containing the names of the local variables (starting with the argument names); `co_cellvars` is a tuple containing the names of local variables that are referenced by nested functions; `co_freevars` is a tuple containing the names of free variables; `co_code` is a string representing the sequence of bytecode instructions; `co_consts` is a tuple containing the literals used by the bytecode; `co_names` is a tuple containing the names used by the bytecode; `co_filename` is the filename from which the code was compiled; `co_firstlineno` is the first line number of the function; `co_lnotab` is a string encoding the mapping from bytecode offsets to line numbers (for details see the source code of the interpreter); `co_stacksize` is the required stack size (including local variables); `co_flags` is an integer encoding a number of flags for the interpreter.

The following flag bits are defined for `co_flags`: bit `0x04` is set if the function uses the `*arguments` syntax to accept an arbitrary number of positional arguments; bit `0x08` is set if the function uses the `**keywords` syntax to accept arbitrary keyword arguments; bit `0x20` is set if the function is a generator.

Future feature declarations (`from __future__ import division`) also use bits in `co_flags` to indicate whether a code object was compiled with a particular feature enabled: bit `0x2000` is set if the function was compiled with future division enabled; bits `0x10` and `0x1000` were used in earlier versions of Python.

Other bits in `co_flags` are reserved for internal use.

If a code object represents a function, the first item in `co_consts` is the documentation string of the function, or `None` if undefined.

Frame objects Frame objects represent execution frames. They may occur in traceback objects (see below).

Special read-only attributes: `f_back` is to the previous stack frame (towards the caller), or `None` if this is the bottom stack frame; `f_code` is the code object being executed in this frame; `f_locals` is the dictionary used to look up local variables; `f_globals` is used for global variables; `f_builtins` is used for built-in (intrinsic) names; `f_restricted` is a flag indicating whether the function is executing in restricted execution mode; `f_lasti` gives the precise instruction (this is an index into the bytecode string of the code object).

Special writable attributes: `f_trace`, if not `None`, is a function called at the start of each source code line (this is used by the debugger); `f_exc_type`, `f_exc_value`, `f_exc_traceback` represent the last exception raised in the parent frame provided another exception was ever raised in the current frame (in all other cases they are None); `f_lineno` is the current line number of the frame — writing to this from within a trace function jumps to the given line (only for the bottom-most frame). A debugger can implement a Jump command (aka Set Next Statement) by writing to f_lineno.

Traceback objects Traceback objects represent a stack trace of an exception. A traceback object is created when an exception occurs. When the search for an exception handler unwinds the execution stack, at each unwound level a traceback object is inserted in front of the current traceback. When an exception handler is entered, the stack trace is made available to the program. (See section *The try statement*.) It is accessible as `sys.exc_traceback`, and also as the third item of the tuple returned by `sys.exc_info()`. The latter is the preferred interface, since it works correctly when the program is using multiple threads. When the program contains no suitable handler, the stack trace is written (nicely formatted) to the standard error stream; if the interpreter is interactive, it is also made available to the user as `sys.last_traceback`.

Special read-only attributes: `tb_next` is the next level in the stack trace (towards the frame where the exception occurred), or `None` if there is no next level; `tb_frame` points to the execution frame of the current level; `tb_lineno` gives the line number where the exception occurred; `tb_lasti` indicates the precise instruction. The line number and last instruction in the traceback may differ from the line number of its frame object if the exception occurred in a `try` statement with no matching except clause or with a finally clause.

Slice objects Slice objects are used to represent slices when *extended slice syntax* is used. This is a slice using two colons, or multiple slices or ellipses separated by commas, e.g., `a[i:j:step]`, `a[i:j, k:l]`, or `a[..., i:j]`. They are also created by the built-in `slice()` function.

Special read-only attributes: `start` is the lower bound; `stop` is the upper bound; `step` is the step value; each is `None` if omitted. These attributes can have any type.

Slice objects support one method:

`slice.`**`indices`**`(self, length)`

This method takes a single integer argument *length* and computes information about the extended slice that the slice object would describe if applied to a sequence of *length* items. It returns a tuple of three integers; respectively these are the *start* and *stop* indices and the *step* or stride length of the slice. Missing or out-of-bounds indices are handled in a manner consistent with regular slices.

New in version 2.3.

Static method objects Static method objects provide a way of defeating the transformation of function objects to method objects described above. A static method object is a wrapper around any other object, usually a user-defined method object. When a static method object is retrieved from a class or a class instance, the object actually returned is the wrapped object, which is not subject to any further transformation. Static method objects are not themselves callable, although the objects they wrap usually are. Static method objects are created by the built-in `staticmethod()` constructor.

Class method objects A class method object, like a static method object, is a wrapper around another object that alters the way in which that object is retrieved from classes and class instances. The behaviour of class method objects upon such retrieval is described above, under "User-defined methods". Class method objects are created by the built-in `classmethod()` constructor.

3.3 New-style and classic classes

Classes and instances come in two flavors: old-style (or classic) and new-style.

Up to Python 2.1 the concept of `class` was unrelated to the concept of `type`, and old-style classes were the only flavor available. For an old-style class, the statement `x.__class__` provides the class of x, but `type(x)` is always `<type 'instance'>`. This reflects the fact that all old-style instances, independent of their class, are implemented with a single built-in type, called `instance`.

New-style classes were introduced in Python 2.2 to unify the concepts of `class` and `type`. A new-style class is simply a user-defined type, no more, no less. If x is an instance of a new-style class, then `type(x)` is typically the same as `x.__class__` (although this is not guaranteed – a new-style class instance is permitted to override the value returned for `x.__class__`).

The major motivation for introducing new-style classes is to provide a unified object model with a full meta-model. It also has a number of practical benefits, like the ability to subclass most built-in types, or the introduction of "descriptors", which enable computed properties.

For compatibility reasons, classes are still old-style by default. New-style classes are created by specifying another new-style class (i.e. a type) as a parent class, or the "top-level type" `object` if no other parent is needed. The behaviour of new-style classes differs from that of old-style classes in a number of important details in addition to what `type()` returns. Some of these changes are fundamental to the new object model, like the way special methods are invoked. Others are "fixes" that could not be implemented before for compatibility concerns, like the method resolution order in case of multiple inheritance.

While this manual aims to provide comprehensive coverage of Python's class mechanics, it may still be lacking in some areas when it comes to its coverage of new-style classes. Please see https://www.python.org/doc/newstyle/ for sources of additional information.

Old-style classes are removed in Python 3, leaving only new-style classes.

3.4 Special method names

A class can implement certain operations that are invoked by special syntax (such as arithmetic operations or subscripting and slicing) by defining methods with special names. This is Python's approach to *operator overloading*, allowing classes to define their own behavior with respect to language operators. For instance, if a class defines a method named `__getitem__()`, and x is an instance of this class, then `x[i]` is roughly equivalent to `x.__getitem__(i)` for old-style classes and `type(x).__getitem__(x, i)` for new-style classes. Except where mentioned, attempts to execute an operation raise an exception when no appropriate method is defined (typically `AttributeError` or `TypeError`).

When implementing a class that emulates any built-in type, it is important that the emulation only be implemented to the degree that it makes sense for the object being modelled. For example, some sequences may work well with retrieval of individual elements, but extracting a slice may not make sense. (One example of this is the `NodeList` interface in the W3C's Document Object Model.)

3.4.1 Basic customization

`object.__new__(cls[, ...])`

> Called to create a new instance of class *cls*. `__new__()` is a static method (special-cased so you need not declare it as such) that takes the class of which an instance was requested as its first argument. The remaining arguments are those passed to the object constructor expression (the call to the class). The return value of `__new__()` should be the new object instance (usually an instance of *cls*).

Typical implementations create a new instance of the class by invoking the superclass's __new__() method using super(currentclass, cls).__new__(cls[, ...]) with appropriate arguments and then modifying the newly-created instance as necessary before returning it.

If __new__() returns an instance of *cls*, then the new instance's __init__() method will be invoked like __init__(self[, ...]), where *self* is the new instance and the remaining arguments are the same as were passed to __new__().

If __new__() does not return an instance of *cls*, then the new instance's __init__() method will not be invoked.

__new__() is intended mainly to allow subclasses of immutable types (like int, str, or tuple) to customize instance creation. It is also commonly overridden in custom metaclasses in order to customize class creation.

object.**__init__**(*self*[, ...])
Called after the instance has been created (by __new__()), but before it is returned to the caller. The arguments are those passed to the class constructor expression. If a base class has an __init__() method, the derived class's __init__() method, if any, must explicitly call it to ensure proper initialization of the base class part of the instance; for example: BaseClass.__init__(self, [args...]).

Because __new__() and __init__() work together in constructing objects (__new__() to create it, and __init__() to customise it), no non-None value may be returned by __init__(); doing so will cause a TypeError to be raised at runtime.

object.**__del__**(*self*)
Called when the instance is about to be destroyed. This is also called a destructor. If a base class has a __del__() method, the derived class's __del__() method, if any, must explicitly call it to ensure proper deletion of the base class part of the instance. Note that it is possible (though not recommended!) for the __del__() method to postpone destruction of the instance by creating a new reference to it. It may then be called at a later time when this new reference is deleted. It is not guaranteed that __del__() methods are called for objects that still exist when the interpreter exits.

Note: del x doesn't directly call x.__del__() — the former decrements the reference count for x by one, and the latter is only called when x's reference count reaches zero. Some common situations that may prevent the reference count of an object from going to zero include: circular references between objects (e.g., a doubly-linked list or a tree data structure with parent and child pointers); a reference to the object on the stack frame of a function that caught an exception (the traceback stored in sys.exc_traceback keeps the stack frame alive); or a reference to the object on the stack frame that raised an unhandled exception in interactive mode (the traceback stored in sys.last_traceback keeps the stack frame alive). The first situation can only be remedied by explicitly breaking the cycles; the latter two situations can be resolved by storing None in sys.exc_traceback or sys.last_traceback. Circular references which are garbage are detected when the option cycle detector is enabled (it's on by default), but can only be cleaned up if there are no Python-level __del__() methods involved. Refer to the documentation for the gc module for more information about how __del__() methods are handled by the cycle detector, particularly the description of the garbage value.

Warning: Due to the precarious circumstances under which __del__() methods are invoked, exceptions that occur during their execution are ignored, and a warning is printed to sys.stderr instead. Also, when __del__() is invoked in response to a module being deleted (e.g., when execution of the program is done), other globals referenced by the __del__() method may already have been deleted or in the process of being torn down (e.g. the import machinery shutting down). For this reason, __del__() methods should do the absolute minimum needed to maintain external invariants. Starting with version 1.5, Python guarantees that globals whose name begins with a single underscore are deleted from their module before other globals are deleted; if no other references to such globals exist, this may help in assuring that imported modules are still available at the time when the __del__() method is called.

See also the -R command-line option.

`object.__repr__`(*self*)

Called by the `repr()` built-in function and by string conversions (reverse quotes) to compute the "official" string representation of an object. If at all possible, this should look like a valid Python expression that could be used to recreate an object with the same value (given an appropriate environment). If this is not possible, a string of the form `<...some useful description...>` should be returned. The return value must be a string object. If a class defines `__repr__()` but not `__str__()`, then `__repr__()` is also used when an "informal" string representation of instances of that class is required.

This is typically used for debugging, so it is important that the representation is information-rich and unambiguous.

`object.__str__`(*self*)

Called by the `str()` built-in function and by the `print` statement to compute the "informal" string representation of an object. This differs from `__repr__()` in that it does not have to be a valid Python expression: a more convenient or concise representation may be used instead. The return value must be a string object.

`object.__lt__`(*self, other*)
`object.__le__`(*self, other*)
`object.__eq__`(*self, other*)
`object.__ne__`(*self, other*)
`object.__gt__`(*self, other*)
`object.__ge__`(*self, other*)

New in version 2.1.

These are the so-called "rich comparison" methods, and are called for comparison operators in preference to `__cmp__()` below. The correspondence between operator symbols and method names is as follows: `x<y` calls `x.__lt__(y)`, `x<=y` calls `x.__le__(y)`, `x==y` calls `x.__eq__(y)`, `x!=y` and `x<>y` call `x.__ne__(y)`, `x>y` calls `x.__gt__(y)`, and `x>=y` calls `x.__ge__(y)`.

A rich comparison method may return the singleton `NotImplemented` if it does not implement the operation for a given pair of arguments. By convention, `False` and `True` are returned for a successful comparison. However, these methods can return any value, so if the comparison operator is used in a Boolean context (e.g., in the condition of an `if` statement), Python will call `bool()` on the value to determine if the result is true or false.

There are no implied relationships among the comparison operators. The truth of `x==y` does not imply that `x!=y` is false. Accordingly, when defining `__eq__()`, one should also define `__ne__()` so that the operators will behave as expected. See the paragraph on `__hash__()` for some important notes on creating *hashable* objects which support custom comparison operations and are usable as dictionary keys.

There are no swapped-argument versions of these methods (to be used when the left argument does not support the operation but the right argument does); rather, `__lt__()` and `__gt__()` are each other's reflection, `__le__()` and `__ge__()` are each other's reflection, and `__eq__()` and `__ne__()` are their own reflection.

Arguments to rich comparison methods are never coerced.

To automatically generate ordering operations from a single root operation, see `functools.total_ordering()`.

`object.__cmp__`(*self, other*)

Called by comparison operations if rich comparison (see above) is not defined. Should return a negative integer if `self < other`, zero if `self == other`, a positive integer if `self > other`. If no `__cmp__()`, `__eq__()` or `__ne__()` operation is defined, class instances are compared by object identity ("address"). See also the description of `__hash__()` for some important notes on creating *hashable* objects which support custom comparison operations and are usable as dictionary keys. (Note: the restriction that exceptions are not propagated by `__cmp__()` has been removed since Python 1.5.)

object.__**rcmp**__(*self*, *other*)
>   Changed in version 2.1: No longer supported.

object.__**hash**__(*self*)
>   Called by built-in function hash() and for operations on members of hashed collections including set, frozenset, and dict. __hash__() should return an integer. The only required property is that objects which compare equal have the same hash value; it is advised to somehow mix together (e.g. using exclusive or) the hash values for the components of the object that also play a part in comparison of objects.

>   If a class does not define a __cmp__() or __eq__() method it should not define a __hash__() operation either; if it defines __cmp__() or __eq__() but not __hash__(), its instances will not be usable in hashed collections. If a class defines mutable objects and implements a __cmp__() or __eq__() method, it should not implement __hash__(), since hashable collection implementations require that a object's hash value is immutable (if the object's hash value changes, it will be in the wrong hash bucket).

>   User-defined classes have __cmp__() and __hash__() methods by default; with them, all objects compare unequal (except with themselves) and x.__hash__() returns a result derived from id(x).

>   Classes which inherit a __hash__() method from a parent class but change the meaning of __cmp__() or __eq__() such that the hash value returned is no longer appropriate (e.g. by switching to a value-based concept of equality instead of the default identity based equality) can explicitly flag themselves as being unhashable by setting __hash__ = None in the class definition. Doing so means that not only will instances of the class raise an appropriate TypeError when a program attempts to retrieve their hash value, but they will also be correctly identified as unhashable when checking isinstance(obj, collections.Hashable) (unlike classes which define their own __hash__() to explicitly raise TypeError).

>   Changed in version 2.5: __hash__() may now also return a long integer object; the 32-bit integer is then derived from the hash of that object.

>   Changed in version 2.6: __hash__ may now be set to None to explicitly flag instances of a class as unhashable.

object.__**nonzero**__(*self*)
>   Called to implement truth value testing and the built-in operation bool(); should return False or True, or their integer equivalents 0 or 1. When this method is not defined, __len__() is called, if it is defined, and the object is considered true if its result is nonzero. If a class defines neither __len__() nor __nonzero__(), all its instances are considered true.

object.__**unicode**__(*self*)
>   Called to implement unicode() built-in; should return a Unicode object. When this method is not defined, string conversion is attempted, and the result of string conversion is converted to Unicode using the system default encoding.

3.4.2 Customizing attribute access

The following methods can be defined to customize the meaning of attribute access (use of, assignment to, or deletion of x.name) for class instances.

object.__**getattr**__(*self*, *name*)
>   Called when an attribute lookup has not found the attribute in the usual places (i.e. it is not an instance attribute nor is it found in the class tree for self). name is the attribute name. This method should return the (computed) attribute value or raise an AttributeError exception.

>   Note that if the attribute is found through the normal mechanism, __getattr__() is not called. (This is an intentional asymmetry between __getattr__() and __setattr__().) This is done both for efficiency reasons and because otherwise __getattr__() would have no way to access other attributes of the instance. Note that at least for instance variables, you can fake total control by not inserting any values in the instance attribute dictionary (but instead inserting them in another object). See the __getattribute__() method below for a way to actually get total control in new-style classes.

`object.`**`__setattr__`**`(self, name, value)`

> Called when an attribute assignment is attempted. This is called instead of the normal mechanism (i.e. store the value in the instance dictionary). *name* is the attribute name, *value* is the value to be assigned to it.
>
> If `__setattr__()` wants to assign to an instance attribute, it should not simply execute `self.name = value` — this would cause a recursive call to itself. Instead, it should insert the value in the dictionary of instance attributes, e.g., `self.__dict__[name] = value`. For new-style classes, rather than accessing the instance dictionary, it should call the base class method with the same name, for example, `object.__setattr__(self, name, value)`.

`object.`**`__delattr__`**`(self, name)`

> Like `__setattr__()` but for attribute deletion instead of assignment. This should only be implemented if `del obj.name` is meaningful for the object.

More attribute access for new-style classes

The following methods only apply to new-style classes.

`object.`**`__getattribute__`**`(self, name)`

> Called unconditionally to implement attribute accesses for instances of the class. If the class also defines `__getattr__()`, the latter will not be called unless `__getattribute__()` either calls it explicitly or raises an `AttributeError`. This method should return the (computed) attribute value or raise an `AttributeError` exception. In order to avoid infinite recursion in this method, its implementation should always call the base class method with the same name to access any attributes it needs, for example, `object.__getattribute__(self, name)`.

> **Note:** This method may still be bypassed when looking up special methods as the result of implicit invocation via language syntax or built-in functions. See *Special method lookup for new-style classes*.

Implementing Descriptors

The following methods only apply when an instance of the class containing the method (a so-called *descriptor* class) appears in an *owner* class (the descriptor must be in either the owner's class dictionary or in the class dictionary for one of its parents). In the examples below, "the attribute" refers to the attribute whose name is the key of the property in the owner class' `__dict__`.

`object.`**`__get__`**`(self, instance, owner)`

> Called to get the attribute of the owner class (class attribute access) or of an instance of that class (instance attribute access). *owner* is always the owner class, while *instance* is the instance that the attribute was accessed through, or `None` when the attribute is accessed through the *owner*. This method should return the (computed) attribute value or raise an `AttributeError` exception.

`object.`**`__set__`**`(self, instance, value)`

> Called to set the attribute on an instance *instance* of the owner class to a new value, *value*.

`object.`**`__delete__`**`(self, instance)`

> Called to delete the attribute on an instance *instance* of the owner class.

Invoking Descriptors

In general, a descriptor is an object attribute with "binding behavior", one whose attribute access has been overridden by methods in the descriptor protocol: `__get__()`, `__set__()`, and `__delete__()`. If any of those methods are defined for an object, it is said to be a descriptor.

The default behavior for attribute access is to get, set, or delete the attribute from an object's dictionary. For instance, `a.x` has a lookup chain starting with `a.__dict__['x']`, then `type(a).__dict__['x']`, and continuing through the base classes of `type(a)` excluding metaclasses.

However, if the looked-up value is an object defining one of the descriptor methods, then Python may override the default behavior and invoke the descriptor method instead. Where this occurs in the precedence chain depends on which descriptor methods were defined and how they were called. Note that descriptors are only invoked for new style objects or classes (ones that subclass `object()` or `type()`).

The starting point for descriptor invocation is a binding, `a.x`. How the arguments are assembled depends on `a`:

Direct Call The simplest and least common call is when user code directly invokes a descriptor method: `x.__get__(a)`.

Instance Binding If binding to a new-style object instance, `a.x` is transformed into the call: `type(a).__dict__['x'].__get__(a, type(a))`.

Class Binding If binding to a new-style class, `A.x` is transformed into the call: `A.__dict__['x'].__get__(None, A)`.

Super Binding If `a` is an instance of `super`, then the binding `super(B, obj).m()` searches `obj.__class__.__mro__` for the base class `A` immediately preceding `B` and then invokes the descriptor with the call: `A.__dict__['m'].__get__(obj, obj.__class__)`.

For instance bindings, the precedence of descriptor invocation depends on the which descriptor methods are defined. A descriptor can define any combination of `__get__()`, `__set__()` and `__delete__()`. If it does not define `__get__()`, then accessing the attribute will return the descriptor object itself unless there is a value in the object's instance dictionary. If the descriptor defines `__set__()` and/or `__delete__()`, it is a data descriptor; if it defines neither, it is a non-data descriptor. Normally, data descriptors define both `__get__()` and `__set__()`, while non-data descriptors have just the `__get__()` method. Data descriptors with `__set__()` and `__get__()` defined always override a redefinition in an instance dictionary. In contrast, non-data descriptors can be overridden by instances.

Python methods (including `staticmethod()` and `classmethod()`) are implemented as non-data descriptors. Accordingly, instances can redefine and override methods. This allows individual instances to acquire behaviors that differ from other instances of the same class.

The `property()` function is implemented as a data descriptor. Accordingly, instances cannot override the behavior of a property.

__slots__

By default, instances of both old and new-style classes have a dictionary for attribute storage. This wastes space for objects having very few instance variables. The space consumption can become acute when creating large numbers of instances.

The default can be overridden by defining *__slots__* in a new-style class definition. The *__slots__* declaration takes a sequence of instance variables and reserves just enough space in each instance to hold a value for each variable. Space is saved because *__dict__* is not created for each instance.

__slots__

  This class variable can be assigned a string, iterable, or sequence of strings with variable names used by instances. If defined in a new-style class, *__slots__* reserves space for the declared variables and prevents the automatic creation of *__dict__* and *__weakref__* for each instance.

  New in version 2.2.

Notes on using *__slots__*

3.4. Special method names   **29**

- When inheriting from a class without __*slots*__, the __*dict*__ attribute of that class will always be accessible, so a __*slots*__ definition in the subclass is meaningless.

- Without a __*dict*__ variable, instances cannot be assigned new variables not listed in the __*slots*__ definition. Attempts to assign to an unlisted variable name raises `AttributeError`. If dynamic assignment of new variables is desired, then add `'__dict__'` to the sequence of strings in the __*slots*__ declaration.

  Changed in version 2.3: Previously, adding `'__dict__'` to the __*slots*__ declaration would not enable the assignment of new attributes not specifically listed in the sequence of instance variable names.

- Without a __*weakref*__ variable for each instance, classes defining __*slots*__ do not support weak references to its instances. If weak reference support is needed, then add `'__weakref__'` to the sequence of strings in the __*slots*__ declaration.

  Changed in version 2.3: Previously, adding `'__weakref__'` to the __*slots*__ declaration would not enable support for weak references.

- __*slots*__ are implemented at the class level by creating descriptors (*Implementing Descriptors*) for each variable name. As a result, class attributes cannot be used to set default values for instance variables defined by __*slots*__; otherwise, the class attribute would overwrite the descriptor assignment.

- The action of a __*slots*__ declaration is limited to the class where it is defined. As a result, subclasses will have a __*dict*__ unless they also define __*slots*__ (which must only contain names of any *additional* slots).

- If a class defines a slot also defined in a base class, the instance variable defined by the base class slot is inaccessible (except by retrieving its descriptor directly from the base class). This renders the meaning of the program undefined. In the future, a check may be added to prevent this.

- Nonempty __*slots*__ does not work for classes derived from "variable-length" built-in types such as `long`, `str` and `tuple`.

- Any non-string iterable may be assigned to __*slots*__. Mappings may also be used; however, in the future, special meaning may be assigned to the values corresponding to each key.

- __*class*__ assignment works only if both classes have the same __*slots*__.

  Changed in version 2.6: Previously, __*class*__ assignment raised an error if either new or old class had __*slots*__.

3.4.3 Customizing class creation

By default, new-style classes are constructed using `type()`. A class definition is read into a separate namespace and the value of class name is bound to the result of `type(name, bases, dict)`.

When the class definition is read, if __*metaclass*__ is defined then the callable assigned to it will be called instead of `type()`. This allows classes or functions to be written which monitor or alter the class creation process:

- Modifying the class dictionary prior to the class being created.

- Returning an instance of another class – essentially performing the role of a factory function.

These steps will have to be performed in the metaclass's `__new__()` method – `type.__new__()` can then be called from this method to create a class with different properties. This example adds a new element to the class dictionary before creating the class:

```python
class metacls(type):
    def __new__(mcs, name, bases, dict):
        dict['foo'] = 'metacls was here'
        return type.__new__(mcs, name, bases, dict)
```

You can of course also override other class methods (or add new methods); for example defining a custom `__call__()` method in the metaclass allows custom behavior when the class is called, e.g. not always creating a new instance.

__metaclass__
>   This variable can be any callable accepting arguments for `name`, `bases`, and `dict`. Upon class creation, the callable is used instead of the built-in `type()`.
>
>   New in version 2.2.

The appropriate metaclass is determined by the following precedence rules:

- If `dict['__metaclass__']` exists, it is used.

- Otherwise, if there is at least one base class, its metaclass is used (this looks for a *__class__* attribute first and if not found, uses its type).

- Otherwise, if a global variable named __metaclass__ exists, it is used.

- Otherwise, the old-style, classic metaclass (types.ClassType) is used.

The potential uses for metaclasses are boundless. Some ideas that have been explored including logging, interface checking, automatic delegation, automatic property creation, proxies, frameworks, and automatic resource locking/synchronization.

3.4.4 Customizing instance and subclass checks

New in version 2.6.

The following methods are used to override the default behavior of the `isinstance()` and `issubclass()` built-in functions.

In particular, the metaclass `abc.ABCMeta` implements these methods in order to allow the addition of Abstract Base Classes (ABCs) as "virtual base classes" to any class or type (including built-in types), including other ABCs.

`class.`**`__instancecheck__`**`(self, instance)`
>   Return true if *instance* should be considered a (direct or indirect) instance of *class*. If defined, called to implement `isinstance(instance, class)`.

`class.`**`__subclasscheck__`**`(self, subclass)`
>   Return true if *subclass* should be considered a (direct or indirect) subclass of *class*. If defined, called to implement `issubclass(subclass, class)`.

Note that these methods are looked up on the type (metaclass) of a class. They cannot be defined as class methods in the actual class. This is consistent with the lookup of special methods that are called on instances, only in this case the instance is itself a class.

See also:

PEP 3119 - Introducing Abstract Base Classes Includes the specification for customizing `isinstance()` and `issubclass()` behavior through `__instancecheck__()` and `__subclasscheck__()`, with motivation for this functionality in the context of adding Abstract Base Classes (see the `abc` module) to the language.

3.4.5 Emulating callable objects

`object.`**`__call__`**`(self[, args...])`
>   Called when the instance is "called" as a function; if this method is defined, `x(arg1, arg2, ...)` is a shorthand for `x.__call__(arg1, arg2, ...)`.

3.4.6 Emulating container types

The following methods can be defined to implement container objects. Containers usually are sequences (such as lists or tuples) or mappings (like dictionaries), but can represent other containers as well. The first set of methods is used either to emulate a sequence or to emulate a mapping; the difference is that for a sequence, the allowable keys should be the integers k for which $0 \;<=\; k \;<\; N$ where N is the length of the sequence, or slice objects, which define a range of items. (For backwards compatibility, the method __getslice__() (see below) can also be defined to handle simple, but not extended slices.) It is also recommended that mappings provide the methods keys(), values(), items(), has_key(), get(), clear(), setdefault(), iterkeys(), itervalues(), iteritems(), pop(), popitem(), copy(), and update() behaving similar to those for Python's standard dictionary objects. The UserDict module provides a DictMixin class to help create those methods from a base set of __getitem__(), __setitem__(), __delitem__(), and keys(). Mutable sequences should provide methods append(), count(), index(), extend(), insert(), pop(), remove(), reverse() and sort(), like Python standard list objects. Finally, sequence types should implement addition (meaning concatenation) and multiplication (meaning repetition) by defining the methods __add__(), __radd__(), __iadd__(), __mul__(), __rmul__() and __imul__() described below; they should not define __coerce__() or other numerical operators. It is recommended that both mappings and sequences implement the __contains__() method to allow efficient use of the in operator; for mappings, in should be equivalent of has_key(); for sequences, it should search through the values. It is further recommended that both mappings and sequences implement the __iter__() method to allow efficient iteration through the container; for mappings, __iter__() should be the same as iterkeys(); for sequences, it should iterate through the values.

object.**__len__**(*self*)

   Called to implement the built-in function len(). Should return the length of the object, an integer >= 0. Also, an object that doesn't define a __nonzero__() method and whose __len__() method returns zero is considered to be false in a Boolean context.

object.**__getitem__**(*self, key*)

   Called to implement evaluation of self[key]. For sequence types, the accepted keys should be integers and slice objects. Note that the special interpretation of negative indexes (if the class wishes to emulate a sequence type) is up to the __getitem__() method. If *key* is of an inappropriate type, TypeError may be raised; if of a value outside the set of indexes for the sequence (after any special interpretation of negative values), IndexError should be raised. For mapping types, if *key* is missing (not in the container), KeyError should be raised.

   Note: for loops expect that an IndexError will be raised for illegal indexes to allow proper detection of the end of the sequence.

---

object.**__missing__**(*self, key*)

   Called by dict.__getitem__() to implement self[key] for dict subclasses when key is not in the dictionary.

object.**__setitem__**(*self, key, value*)

   Called to implement assignment to self[key]. Same note as for __getitem__(). This should only be implemented for mappings if the objects support changes to the values for keys, or if new keys can be added, or for sequences if elements can be replaced. The same exceptions should be raised for improper *key* values as for the __getitem__() method.

object.**__delitem__**(*self, key*)

   Called to implement deletion of self[key]. Same note as for __getitem__(). This should only be implemented for mappings if the objects support removal of keys, or for sequences if elements can be removed from the sequence. The same exceptions should be raised for improper *key* values as for the __getitem__() method.

object.**__iter__**(*self*)

   This method is called when an iterator is required for a container. This method should return a new iterator object that can iterate over all the objects in the container. For mappings, it should iterate over the keys of the container, and should also be made available as the method `iterkeys()`.

Iterator objects also need to implement this method; they are required to return themselves. For more information on iterator objects, see *typeiter*.

object.**__reversed__**(*self*)

Called (if present) by the `reversed()` built-in to implement reverse iteration. It should return a new iterator object that iterates over all the objects in the container in reverse order.

If the `__reversed__()` method is not provided, the `reversed()` built-in will fall back to using the sequence protocol (`__len__()` and `__getitem__()`). Objects that support the sequence protocol should only provide `__reversed__()` if they can provide an implementation that is more efficient than the one provided by `reversed()`.

New in version 2.6.

The membership test operators (`in` and `not in`) are normally implemented as an iteration through a sequence. However, container objects can supply the following special method with a more efficient implementation, which also does not require the object be a sequence.

object.**__contains__**(*self*, *item*)

Called to implement membership test operators. Should return true if *item* is in *self*, false otherwise. For mapping objects, this should consider the keys of the mapping rather than the values or the key-item pairs.

For objects that don't define `__contains__()`, the membership test first tries iteration via `__iter__()`, then the old sequence iteration protocol via `__getitem__()`, see *this section in the language reference*.

3.4.7 Additional methods for emulation of sequence types

The following optional methods can be defined to further emulate sequence objects. Immutable sequences methods should at most only define `__getslice__()`; mutable sequences might define all three methods.

object.**__getslice__**(*self*, *i*, *j*)

Deprecated since version 2.0: Support slice objects as parameters to the `__getitem__()` method. (However, built-in types in CPython currently still implement `__getslice__()`. Therefore, you have to override it in derived classes when implementing slicing.)

Called to implement evaluation of `self[i:j]`. The returned object should be of the same type as *self*. Note that missing *i* or *j* in the slice expression are replaced by zero or `sys.maxsize`, respectively. If negative indexes are used in the slice, the length of the sequence is added to that index. If the instance does not implement the `__len__()` method, an `AttributeError` is raised. No guarantee is made that indexes adjusted this way are not still negative. Indexes which are greater than the length of the sequence are not modified. If no `__getslice__()` is found, a slice object is created instead, and passed to `__getitem__()` instead.

object.**__setslice__**(*self*, *i*, *j*, *sequence*)

Called to implement assignment to `self[i:j]`. Same notes for *i* and *j* as for `__getslice__()`.

This method is deprecated. If no `__setslice__()` is found, or for extended slicing of the form `self[i:j:k]`, a slice object is created, and passed to `__setitem__()`, instead of `__setslice__()` being called.

object.**__delslice__**(*self*, *i*, *j*)

Called to implement deletion of `self[i:j]`. Same notes for *i* and *j* as for `__getslice__()`. This method is deprecated. If no `__delslice__()` is found, or for extended slicing of the form `self[i:j:k]`, a slice object is created, and passed to `__delitem__()`, instead of `__delslice__()` being called.

Notice that these methods are only invoked when a single slice with a single colon is used, and the slice method is available. For slice operations involving extended slice notation, or in absence of the slice methods, `__getitem__()`, `__setitem__()` or `__delitem__()` is called with a slice object as argument.

The following example demonstrate how to make your program or module compatible with earlier versions of Python (assuming that methods __getitem__(), __setitem__() and __delitem__() support slice objects as arguments):

```
class MyClass:
    ...
    def __getitem__(self, index):
        ...
    def __setitem__(self, index, value):
        ...
    def __delitem__(self, index):
        ...

    if sys.version_info < (2, 0):
        # They won't be defined if version is at least 2.0 final

        def __getslice__(self, i, j):
            return self[max(0, i):max(0, j):]
        def __setslice__(self, i, j, seq):
            self[max(0, i):max(0, j):] = seq
        def __delslice__(self, i, j):
            del self[max(0, i):max(0, j):]
    ...
```

Note the calls to max(); these are necessary because of the handling of negative indices before the __*slice__() methods are called. When negative indexes are used, the __*item__() methods receive them as provided, but the __*slice__() methods get a "cooked" form of the index values. For each negative index value, the length of the sequence is added to the index before calling the method (which may still result in a negative index); this is the customary handling of negative indexes by the built-in sequence types, and the __*item__() methods are expected to do this as well. However, since they should already be doing that, negative indexes cannot be passed in; they must be constrained to the bounds of the sequence before being passed to the __*item__() methods. Calling max(0, i) conveniently returns the proper value.

3.4.8 Emulating numeric types

The following methods can be defined to emulate numeric objects. Methods corresponding to operations that are not supported by the particular kind of number implemented (e.g., bitwise operations for non-integral numbers) should be left undefined.

object.**__add__**(*self, other*)
object.**__sub__**(*self, other*)
object.**__mul__**(*self, other*)
object.**__floordiv__**(*self, other*)
object.**__mod__**(*self, other*)
object.**__divmod__**(*self, other*)
object.**__pow__**(*self, other*[, *modulo*])
object.**__lshift__**(*self, other*)
object.**__rshift__**(*self, other*)
object.**__and__**(*self, other*)
object.**__xor__**(*self, other*)
object.**__or__**(*self, other*)

These methods are called to implement the binary arithmetic operations (+, -, *, //, %, divmod(), pow(), **, <<, >>, &, ^, |). For instance, to evaluate the expression x + y, where x is an instance of a class that has an __add__() method, x.__add__(y) is called. The __divmod__() method should be the equivalent to using __floordiv__() and __mod__(); it should not be related to __truediv__() (described below).

Note that `__pow__()` should be defined to accept an optional third argument if the ternary version of the built-in `pow()` function is to be supported.

If one of those methods does not support the operation with the supplied arguments, it should return `NotImplemented`.

`object.`**`__div__`**`(self, other)`
`object.`**`__truediv__`**`(self, other)`
> The division operator (`/`) is implemented by these methods. The `__truediv__()` method is used when `__future__.division` is in effect, otherwise `__div__()` is used. If only one of these two methods is defined, the object will not support division in the alternate context; `TypeError` will be raised instead.

`object.`**`__radd__`**`(self, other)`
`object.`**`__rsub__`**`(self, other)`
`object.`**`__rmul__`**`(self, other)`
`object.`**`__rdiv__`**`(self, other)`
`object.`**`__rtruediv__`**`(self, other)`
`object.`**`__rfloordiv__`**`(self, other)`
`object.`**`__rmod__`**`(self, other)`
`object.`**`__rdivmod__`**`(self, other)`
`object.`**`__rpow__`**`(self, other)`
`object.`**`__rlshift__`**`(self, other)`
`object.`**`__rrshift__`**`(self, other)`
`object.`**`__rand__`**`(self, other)`
`object.`**`__rxor__`**`(self, other)`
`object.`**`__ror__`**`(self, other)`
> These methods are called to implement the binary arithmetic operations (`+`, `-`, `*`, `/`, `%`, `divmod()`, `pow()`, `**`, `<<`, `>>`, `&`, `^`, `|`) with reflected (swapped) operands. These functions are only called if the left operand does not support the corresponding operation and the operands are of different types. [2] For instance, to evaluate the expression `x - y`, where `y` is an instance of a class that has an `__rsub__()` method, `y.__rsub__(x)` is called if `x.__sub__(y)` returns *NotImplemented*.
>
> Note that ternary `pow()` will not try calling `__rpow__()` (the coercion rules would become too complicated).

Note: If the right operand's type is a subclass of the left operand's type and that subclass provides the reflected method for the operation, this method will be called before the left operand's non-reflected method. This behavior allows subclasses to override their ancestors' operations.

`object.`**`__iadd__`**`(self, other)`
`object.`**`__isub__`**`(self, other)`
`object.`**`__imul__`**`(self, other)`
`object.`**`__idiv__`**`(self, other)`
`object.`**`__itruediv__`**`(self, other)`
`object.`**`__ifloordiv__`**`(self, other)`
`object.`**`__imod__`**`(self, other)`
`object.`**`__ipow__`**`(self, other[, modulo])`
`object.`**`__ilshift__`**`(self, other)`
`object.`**`__irshift__`**`(self, other)`
`object.`**`__iand__`**`(self, other)`
`object.`**`__ixor__`**`(self, other)`
`object.`**`__ior__`**`(self, other)`
> These methods are called to implement the augmented arithmetic assignments (`+=`, `-=`, `*=`, `/=`, `//=`, `%=`, `**=`, `<<=`, `>>=`, `&=`, `^=`, `|=`). These methods should attempt to do the operation in-place (modifying *self*) and return the result (which could be, but does not have to be, *self*). If a specific method is not defined, the augmented

---

[2] For operands of the same type, it is assumed that if the non-reflected method (such as `__add__()`) fails the operation is not supported, which is why the reflected method is not called.

assignment falls back to the normal methods. For instance, to execute the statement x += y, where *x* is an instance of a class that has an `__iadd__` () method, `x.__iadd__` (y) is called. If *x* is an instance of a class that does not define a `__iadd__` () method, `x.__add__` (y) and `y.__radd__` (x) are considered, as with the evaluation of x + y.

object.**__neg__** (*self*)
object.**__pos__** (*self*)
object.**__abs__** (*self*)
object.**__invert__** (*self*)
>   Called to implement the unary arithmetic operations (−, +, abs () and ~).

object.**__complex__** (*self*)
object.**__int__** (*self*)
object.**__long__** (*self*)
object.**__float__** (*self*)
>   Called to implement the built-in functions complex (), int (), long (), and float (). Should return a value of the appropriate type.

object.**__oct__** (*self*)
object.**__hex__** (*self*)
>   Called to implement the built-in functions oct () and hex (). Should return a string value.

object.**__index__** (*self*)
>   Called to implement operator.index (). Also called whenever Python needs an integer object (such as in slicing). Must return an integer (int or long).
>
>   New in version 2.5.

object.**__coerce__** (*self, other*)
>   Called to implement "mixed-mode" numeric arithmetic. Should either return a 2-tuple containing *self* and *other* converted to a common numeric type, or None if conversion is impossible. When the common type would be the type of other, it is sufficient to return None, since the interpreter will also ask the other object to attempt a coercion (but sometimes, if the implementation of the other type cannot be changed, it is useful to do the conversion to the other type here). A return value of NotImplemented is equivalent to returning None.

3.4.9 Coercion rules

This section used to document the rules for coercion. As the language has evolved, the coercion rules have become hard to document precisely; documenting what one version of one particular implementation does is undesirable. Instead, here are some informal guidelines regarding coercion. In Python 3, coercion will not be supported.

- If the left operand of a % operator is a string or Unicode object, no coercion takes place and the string formatting operation is invoked instead.

- It is no longer recommended to define a coercion operation. Mixed-mode operations on types that don't define coercion pass the original arguments to the operation.

- New-style classes (those derived from object) never invoke the `__coerce__` () method in response to a binary operator; the only time `__coerce__` () is invoked is when the built-in function coerce () is called.

- For most intents and purposes, an operator that returns NotImplemented is treated the same as one that is not implemented at all.

- Below, `__op__` () and `__rop__` () are used to signify the generic method names corresponding to an operator; `__iop__` () is used for the corresponding in-place operator. For example, for the operator '+', `__add__` () and `__radd__` () are used for the left and right variant of the binary operator, and `__iadd__` () for the in-place variant.

- For objects *x* and *y*, first `x.__op__(y)` is tried. If this is not implemented or returns `NotImplemented`, `y.__rop__(x)` is tried. If this is also not implemented or returns `NotImplemented`, a `TypeError` exception is raised. But see the following exception:

- Exception to the previous item: if the left operand is an instance of a built-in type or a new-style class, and the right operand is an instance of a proper subclass of that type or class and overrides the base's `__rop__()` method, the right operand's `__rop__()` method is tried *before* the left operand's `__op__()` method.

  This is done so that a subclass can completely override binary operators. Otherwise, the left operand's `__op__()` method would always accept the right operand: when an instance of a given class is expected, an instance of a subclass of that class is always acceptable.

- When either operand type defines a coercion, this coercion is called before that type's `__op__()` or `__rop__()` method is called, but no sooner. If the coercion returns an object of a different type for the operand whose coercion is invoked, part of the process is redone using the new object.

- When an in-place operator (like '+=') is used, if the left operand implements `__iop__()`, it is invoked without any coercion. When the operation falls back to `__op__()` and/or `__rop__()`, the normal coercion rules apply.

- In `x + y`, if *x* is a sequence that implements sequence concatenation, sequence concatenation is invoked.

- In `x * y`, if one operand is a sequence that implements sequence repetition, and the other is an integer (`int` or `long`), sequence repetition is invoked.

- Rich comparisons (implemented by methods `__eq__()` and so on) never use coercion. Three-way comparison (implemented by `__cmp__()`) does use coercion under the same conditions as other binary operations use it.

- In the current implementation, the built-in numeric types `int`, `long`, `float`, and `complex` do not use coercion. All these types implement a `__coerce__()` method, for use by the built-in `coerce()` function.

  Changed in version 2.7: The complex type no longer makes implicit calls to the `__coerce__()` method for mixed-type binary arithmetic operations.

3.4.10 With Statement Context Managers

New in version 2.5.

A *context manager* is an object that defines the runtime context to be established when executing a `with` statement. The context manager handles the entry into, and the exit from, the desired runtime context for the execution of the block of code. Context managers are normally invoked using the `with` statement (described in section *The with statement*), but can also be used by directly invoking their methods.

Typical uses of context managers include saving and restoring various kinds of global state, locking and unlocking resources, closing opened files, etc.

For more information on context managers, see *typecontextmanager*.

`object.__enter__(self)`
> Enter the runtime context related to this object. The `with` statement will bind this method's return value to the target(s) specified in the `as` clause of the statement, if any.

`object.__exit__(self, exc_type, exc_value, traceback)`
> Exit the runtime context related to this object. The parameters describe the exception that caused the context to be exited. If the context was exited without an exception, all three arguments will be `None`.

> If an exception is supplied, and the method wishes to suppress the exception (i.e., prevent it from being propagated), it should return a true value. Otherwise, the exception will be processed normally upon exit from this method.

> Note that `__exit__()` methods should not reraise the passed-in exception; this is the caller's responsibility.

See also:

PEP 0343 - The "with" statement The specification, background, and examples for the Python `with` statement.

3.4.11 Special method lookup for old-style classes

For old-style classes, special methods are always looked up in exactly the same way as any other method or attribute. This is the case regardless of whether the method is being looked up explicitly as in x.__getitem__(i) or implicitly as in x[i].

This behaviour means that special methods may exhibit different behaviour for different instances of a single old-style class if the appropriate special attributes are set differently:

```
>>> class C:
...     pass
...
>>> c1 = C()
>>> c2 = C()
>>> c1.__len__ = lambda: 5
>>> c2.__len__ = lambda: 9
>>> len(c1)
5
>>> len(c2)
9
```

3.4.12 Special method lookup for new-style classes

For new-style classes, implicit invocations of special methods are only guaranteed to work correctly if defined on an object's type, not in the object's instance dictionary. That behaviour is the reason why the following code raises an exception (unlike the equivalent example with old-style classes):

```
>>> class C(object):
...     pass
...
>>> c = C()
>>> c.__len__ = lambda: 5
>>> len(c)
Traceback (most recent call last):
  File "<stdin>", line 1, in <module>
TypeError: object of type 'C' has no len()
```

The rationale behind this behaviour lies with a number of special methods such as __hash__() and __repr__() that are implemented by all objects, including type objects. If the implicit lookup of these methods used the conventional lookup process, they would fail when invoked on the type object itself:

```
>>> 1 .__hash__() == hash(1)
True
>>> int.__hash__() == hash(int)
Traceback (most recent call last):
  File "<stdin>", line 1, in <module>
TypeError: descriptor '__hash__' of 'int' object needs an argument
```

Incorrectly attempting to invoke an unbound method of a class in this way is sometimes referred to as 'metaclass confusion', and is avoided by bypassing the instance when looking up special methods:

```
>>> type(1).__hash__(1) == hash(1)
True
>>> type(int).__hash__(int) == hash(int)
True
```

In addition to bypassing any instance attributes in the interest of correctness, implicit special method lookup generally also bypasses the __getattribute__() method even of the object's metaclass:

```
>>> class Meta(type):
...     def __getattribute__(*args):
...         print "Metaclass getattribute invoked"
...         return type.__getattribute__(*args)
...
>>> class C(object):
...     __metaclass__ = Meta
...     def __len__(self):
...         return 10
...     def __getattribute__(*args):
...         print "Class getattribute invoked"
...         return object.__getattribute__(*args)
...
>>> c = C()
>>> c.__len__()                 # Explicit lookup via instance
Class getattribute invoked
10
>>> type(c).__len__(c)          # Explicit lookup via type
Metaclass getattribute invoked
10
>>> len(c)                      # Implicit lookup
10
```

Bypassing the __getattribute__() machinery in this fashion provides significant scope for speed optimisations within the interpreter, at the cost of some flexibility in the handling of special methods (the special method *must* be set on the class object itself in order to be consistently invoked by the interpreter).

FOUR

EXECUTION MODEL

4.1 Naming and binding

Names refer to objects. Names are introduced by name binding operations. Each occurrence of a name in the program text refers to the *binding* of that name established in the innermost function block containing the use.

A *block* is a piece of Python program text that is executed as a unit. The following are blocks: a module, a function body, and a class definition. Each command typed interactively is a block. A script file (a file given as standard input to the interpreter or specified on the interpreter command line the first argument) is a code block. A script command (a command specified on the interpreter command line with the '**-c**' option) is a code block. The file read by the built-in function `execfile()` is a code block. The string argument passed to the built-in function `eval()` and to the `exec` statement is a code block. The expression read and evaluated by the built-in function `input()` is a code block.

A code block is executed in an *execution frame*. A frame contains some administrative information (used for debugging) and determines where and how execution continues after the code block's execution has completed.

A *scope* defines the visibility of a name within a block. If a local variable is defined in a block, its scope includes that block. If the definition occurs in a function block, the scope extends to any blocks contained within the defining one, unless a contained block introduces a different binding for the name. The scope of names defined in a class block is limited to the class block; it does not extend to the code blocks of methods – this includes generator expressions since they are implemented using a function scope. This means that the following will fail:

```
class A:
    a = 42
    b = list(a + i for i in range(10))
```

When a name is used in a code block, it is resolved using the nearest enclosing scope. The set of all such scopes visible to a code block is called the block's *environment*.

If a name is bound in a block, it is a local variable of that block. If a name is bound at the module level, it is a global variable. (The variables of the module code block are local and global.) If a variable is used in a code block but not defined there, it is a *free variable*.

When a name is not found at all, a `NameError` exception is raised. If the name refers to a local variable that has not been bound, a `UnboundLocalError` exception is raised. `UnboundLocalError` is a subclass of `NameError`.

The following constructs bind names: formal parameters to functions, `import` statements, class and function definitions (these bind the class or function name in the defining block), and targets that are identifiers if occurring in an assignment, `for` loop header, in the second position of an `except` clause header or after `as` in a `with` statement. The `import` statement of the form `from ... import *` binds all names defined in the imported module, except those beginning with an underscore. This form may only be used at the module level.

A target occurring in a `del` statement is also considered bound for this purpose (though the actual semantics are to unbind the name). It is illegal to unbind a name that is referenced by an enclosing scope; the compiler will report a `SyntaxError`.

Each assignment or import statement occurs within a block defined by a class or function definition or at the module level (the top-level code block).

If a name binding operation occurs anywhere within a code block, all uses of the name within the block are treated as references to the current block. This can lead to errors when a name is used within a block before it is bound. This rule is subtle. Python lacks declarations and allows name binding operations to occur anywhere within a code block. The local variables of a code block can be determined by scanning the entire text of the block for name binding operations.

If the global statement occurs within a block, all uses of the name specified in the statement refer to the binding of that name in the top-level namespace. Names are resolved in the top-level namespace by searching the global namespace, i.e. the namespace of the module containing the code block, and the builtins namespace, the namespace of the module __builtin__. The global namespace is searched first. If the name is not found there, the builtins namespace is searched. The global statement must precede all uses of the name.

The builtins namespace associated with the execution of a code block is actually found by looking up the name __builtins__ in its global namespace; this should be a dictionary or a module (in the latter case the module's dictionary is used). By default, when in the __main__ module, __builtins__ is the built-in module __builtin__ (note: no 's'); when in any other module, __builtins__ is an alias for the dictionary of the __builtin__ module itself. __builtins__ can be set to a user-created dictionary to create a weak form of restricted execution.

CPython implementation detail: Users should not touch __builtins__; it is strictly an implementation detail. Users wanting to override values in the builtins namespace should `import` the __builtin__ (no 's') module and modify its attributes appropriately.

The namespace for a module is automatically created the first time a module is imported. The main module for a script is always called __main__.

The `global` statement has the same scope as a name binding operation in the same block. If the nearest enclosing scope for a free variable contains a global statement, the free variable is treated as a global.

A class definition is an executable statement that may use and define names. These references follow the normal rules for name resolution. The namespace of the class definition becomes the attribute dictionary of the class. Names defined at the class scope are not visible in methods.

4.1.1 Interaction with dynamic features

There are several cases where Python statements are illegal when used in conjunction with nested scopes that contain free variables.

If a variable is referenced in an enclosing scope, it is illegal to delete the name. An error will be reported at compile time.

If the wild card form of import — `import *` — is used in a function and the function contains or is a nested block with free variables, the compiler will raise a `SyntaxError`.

If `exec` is used in a function and the function contains or is a nested block with free variables, the compiler will raise a `SyntaxError` unless the exec explicitly specifies the local namespace for the `exec`. (In other words, `exec obj` would be illegal, but `exec obj in ns` would be legal.)

The `eval()`, `execfile()`, and `input()` functions and the `exec` statement do not have access to the full environment for resolving names. Names may be resolved in the local and global namespaces of the caller. Free variables are not resolved in the nearest enclosing namespace, but in the global namespace. [1] The `exec` statement and the `eval()` and `execfile()` functions have optional arguments to override the global and local namespace. If only one namespace is specified, it is used for both.

---

[1] This limitation occurs because the code that is executed by these operations is not available at the time the module is compiled.

4.2 Exceptions

Exceptions are a means of breaking out of the normal flow of control of a code block in order to handle errors or other exceptional conditions. An exception is *raised* at the point where the error is detected; it may be *handled* by the surrounding code block or by any code block that directly or indirectly invoked the code block where the error occurred.

The Python interpreter raises an exception when it detects a run-time error (such as division by zero). A Python program can also explicitly raise an exception with the `raise` statement. Exception handlers are specified with the `try ... except` statement. The `finally` clause of such a statement can be used to specify cleanup code which does not handle the exception, but is executed whether an exception occurred or not in the preceding code.

Python uses the "termination" model of error handling: an exception handler can find out what happened and continue execution at an outer level, but it cannot repair the cause of the error and retry the failing operation (except by re-entering the offending piece of code from the top).

When an exception is not handled at all, the interpreter terminates execution of the program, or returns to its interactive main loop. In either case, it prints a stack backtrace, except when the exception is `SystemExit`.

Exceptions are identified by class instances. The `except` clause is selected depending on the class of the instance: it must reference the class of the instance or a base class thereof. The instance can be received by the handler and can carry additional information about the exceptional condition.

Exceptions can also be identified by strings, in which case the `except` clause is selected by object identity. An arbitrary value can be raised along with the identifying string which can be passed to the handler.

Note: Messages to exceptions are not part of the Python API. Their contents may change from one version of Python to the next without warning and should not be relied on by code which will run under multiple versions of the interpreter.

See also the description of the `try` statement in section *The try statement* and `raise` statement in section *The raise statement*.

EXPRESSIONS

This chapter explains the meaning of the elements of expressions in Python.

Syntax Notes: In this and the following chapters, extended BNF notation will be used to describe syntax, not lexical analysis. When (one alternative of) a syntax rule has the form

```
name    ::=    othername
```

and no semantics are given, the semantics of this form of `name` are the same as for `othername`.

5.1 Arithmetic conversions

When a description of an arithmetic operator below uses the phrase "the numeric arguments are converted to a common type," the arguments are coerced using the coercion rules listed at *Coercion rules*. If both arguments are standard numeric types, the following coercions are applied:

- If either argument is a complex number, the other is converted to complex;
- otherwise, if either argument is a floating point number, the other is converted to floating point;
- otherwise, if either argument is a long integer, the other is converted to long integer;
- otherwise, both must be plain integers and no conversion is necessary.

Some additional rules apply for certain operators (e.g., a string left argument to the '%' operator). Extensions can define their own coercions.

5.2 Atoms

Atoms are the most basic elements of expressions. The simplest atoms are identifiers or literals. Forms enclosed in reverse quotes or in parentheses, brackets or braces are also categorized syntactically as atoms. The syntax for atoms is:

```
atom        ::=    identifier | literal | enclosure
enclosure   ::=    parenth_form | list_display
                   | generator_expression | dict_display | set_display
                   | string_conversion | yield_atom
```

5.2.1 Identifiers (Names)

An identifier occurring as an atom is a name. See section *Identifiers and keywords* for lexical definition and section *Naming and binding* for documentation of naming and binding.

When the name is bound to an object, evaluation of the atom yields that object. When a name is not bound, an attempt to evaluate it raises a `NameError` exception.

Private name mangling: When an identifier that textually occurs in a class definition begins with two or more underscore characters and does not end in two or more underscores, it is considered a *private name* of that class. Private names are transformed to a longer form before code is generated for them. The transformation inserts the class name, with leading underscores removed and a single underscore inserted, in front of the name. For example, the identifier __spam occurring in a class named Ham will be transformed to _Ham__spam. This transformation is independent of the syntactical context in which the identifier is used. If the transformed name is extremely long (longer than 255 characters), implementation defined truncation may happen. If the class name consists only of underscores, no transformation is done.

5.2.2 Literals

Python supports string literals and various numeric literals:

```
literal   ::=   stringliteral | integer | longinteger
                | floatnumber | imagnumber
```

Evaluation of a literal yields an object of the given type (string, integer, long integer, floating point number, complex number) with the given value. The value may be approximated in the case of floating point and imaginary (complex) literals. See section *Literals* for details.

All literals correspond to immutable data types, and hence the object's identity is less important than its value. Multiple evaluations of literals with the same value (either the same occurrence in the program text or a different occurrence) may obtain the same object or a different object with the same value.

5.2.3 Parenthesized forms

A parenthesized form is an optional expression list enclosed in parentheses:

```
parenth_form   ::=   "(" [expression_list] ")"
```

A parenthesized expression list yields whatever that expression list yields: if the list contains at least one comma, it yields a tuple; otherwise, it yields the single expression that makes up the expression list.

An empty pair of parentheses yields an empty tuple object. Since tuples are immutable, the rules for literals apply (i.e., two occurrences of the empty tuple may or may not yield the same object).

Note that tuples are not formed by the parentheses, but rather by use of the comma operator. The exception is the empty tuple, for which parentheses *are* required — allowing unparenthesized "nothing" in expressions would cause ambiguities and allow common typos to pass uncaught.

5.2.4 List displays

A list display is a possibly empty series of expressions enclosed in square brackets:

```
list_display            ::=    "[" [expression_list | list_comprehension] "]"
list_comprehension      ::=    expression list_for
list_for                ::=    "for" target_list "in" old_expression_list [list_iter]
old_expression_list     ::=    old_expression [("," old_expression)+ [","]]
old_expression          ::=    or_test | old_lambda_expr
list_iter               ::=    list_for | list_if
list_if                 ::=    "if" old_expression [list_iter]
```

A list display yields a new list object. Its contents are specified by providing either a list of expressions or a list comprehension. When a comma-separated list of expressions is supplied, its elements are evaluated from left to right and placed into the list object in that order. When a list comprehension is supplied, it consists of a single expression followed by at least one for clause and zero or more for or if clauses. In this case, the elements of the new list are those that would be produced by considering each of the for or if clauses a block, nesting from left to right, and evaluating the expression to produce a list element each time the innermost block is reached [1].

5.2.5 Displays for sets and dictionaries

For constructing a set or a dictionary Python provides special syntax called "displays", each of them in two flavors:

- either the container contents are listed explicitly, or
- they are computed via a set of looping and filtering instructions, called a *comprehension*.

Common syntax elements for comprehensions are:

```
comprehension   ::=    expression comp_for
comp_for        ::=    "for" target_list "in" or_test [comp_iter]
comp_iter       ::=    comp_for | comp_if
comp_if         ::=    "if" expression_nocond [comp_iter]
```

The comprehension consists of a single expression followed by at least one for clause and zero or more for or if clauses. In this case, the elements of the new container are those that would be produced by considering each of the for or if clauses a block, nesting from left to right, and evaluating the expression to produce an element each time the innermost block is reached.

Note that the comprehension is executed in a separate scope, so names assigned to in the target list don't "leak" in the enclosing scope.

5.2.6 Generator expressions

A generator expression is a compact generator notation in parentheses:

```
generator_expression   ::=    "(" expression comp_for ")"
```

A generator expression yields a new generator object. Its syntax is the same as for comprehensions, except that it is enclosed in parentheses instead of brackets or curly braces.

Variables used in the generator expression are evaluated lazily when the __next__() method is called for generator object (in the same fashion as normal generators). However, the leftmost for clause is immediately evaluated, so that

---

[1] In Python 2.3 and later releases, a list comprehension "leaks" the control variables of each for it contains into the containing scope. However, this behavior is deprecated, and relying on it will not work in Python 3.

an error produced by it can be seen before any other possible error in the code that handles the generator expression. Subsequent `for` clauses cannot be evaluated immediately since they may depend on the previous `for` loop. For example: `(x*y for x in range(10) for y in bar(x))`.

The parentheses can be omitted on calls with only one argument. See section *Calls* for the detail.

5.2.7 Dictionary displays

A dictionary display is a possibly empty series of key/datum pairs enclosed in curly braces:

```
dict_display       ::=  "{" [key_datum_list | dict_comprehension] "}"
key_datum_list     ::=  key_datum ("," key_datum)* [","]
key_datum          ::=  expression ":"  expression
dict_comprehension ::=  expression ":"  expression comp_for
```

A dictionary display yields a new dictionary object.

If a comma-separated sequence of key/datum pairs is given, they are evaluated from left to right to define the entries of the dictionary: each key object is used as a key into the dictionary to store the corresponding datum. This means that you can specify the same key multiple times in the key/datum list, and the final dictionary's value for that key will be the last one given.

A dict comprehension, in contrast to list and set comprehensions, needs two expressions separated with a colon followed by the usual "for" and "if" clauses. When the comprehension is run, the resulting key and value elements are inserted in the new dictionary in the order they are produced.

Restrictions on the types of the key values are listed earlier in section *The standard type hierarchy*. (To summarize, the key type should be *hashable*, which excludes all mutable objects.) Clashes between duplicate keys are not detected; the last datum (textually rightmost in the display) stored for a given key value prevails.

5.2.8 Set displays

A set display is denoted by curly braces and distinguishable from dictionary displays by the lack of colons separating keys and values:

```
set_display ::=  "{" (expression_list | comprehension) "}"
```

A set display yields a new mutable set object, the contents being specified by either a sequence of expressions or a comprehension. When a comma-separated list of expressions is supplied, its elements are evaluated from left to right and added to the set object. When a comprehension is supplied, the set is constructed from the elements resulting from the comprehension.

An empty set cannot be constructed with `{ }`; this literal constructs an empty dictionary.

5.2.9 String conversions

A string conversion is an expression list enclosed in reverse (a.k.a. backward) quotes:

```
string_conversion ::=  "`" expression_list "`"
```

A string conversion evaluates the contained expression list and converts the resulting object into a string according to rules specific to its type.

If the object is a string, a number, `None`, or a tuple, list or dictionary containing only objects whose type is one of these, the resulting string is a valid Python expression which can be passed to the built-in function `eval()` to yield an expression with the same value (or an approximation, if floating point numbers are involved).

(In particular, converting a string adds quotes around it and converts "funny" characters to escape sequences that are safe to print.)

Recursive objects (for example, lists or dictionaries that contain a reference to themselves, directly or indirectly) use `...` to indicate a recursive reference, and the result cannot be passed to `eval()` to get an equal value (`SyntaxError` will be raised instead).

The built-in function `repr()` performs exactly the same conversion in its argument as enclosing it in parentheses and reverse quotes does. The built-in function `str()` performs a similar but more user-friendly conversion.

5.2.10 Yield expressions

```
yield_atom         ::=   "(" yield_expression ")"
yield_expression   ::=   "yield" [expression_list]
```

New in version 2.5.

The `yield` expression is only used when defining a generator function, and can only be used in the body of a function definition. Using a `yield` expression in a function definition is sufficient to cause that definition to create a generator function instead of a normal function.

When a generator function is called, it returns an iterator known as a generator. That generator then controls the execution of a generator function. The execution starts when one of the generator's methods is called. At that time, the execution proceeds to the first `yield` expression, where it is suspended again, returning the value of `expression_list` to generator's caller. By suspended we mean that all local state is retained, including the current bindings of local variables, the instruction pointer, and the internal evaluation stack. When the execution is resumed by calling one of the generator's methods, the function can proceed exactly as if the `yield` expression was just another external call. The value of the `yield` expression after resuming depends on the method which resumed the execution.

All of this makes generator functions quite similar to coroutines; they yield multiple times, they have more than one entry point and their execution can be suspended. The only difference is that a generator function cannot control where should the execution continue after it yields; the control is always transferred to the generator's caller.

Generator-iterator methods

This subsection describes the methods of a generator iterator. They can be used to control the execution of a generator function.

Note that calling any of the generator methods below when the generator is already executing raises a `ValueError` exception.

`generator.`**`next`**`()`
> Starts the execution of a generator function or resumes it at the last executed `yield` expression. When a generator function is resumed with a `next()` method, the current `yield` expression always evaluates to `None`. The execution then continues to the next `yield` expression, where the generator is suspended again, and the value of the `expression_list` is returned to `next()`'s caller. If the generator exits without yielding another value, a `StopIteration` exception is raised.

`generator.`**`send`**`(`*`value`*`)`
> Resumes the execution and "sends" a value into the generator function. The `value` argument becomes the

result of the current `yield` expression. The `send()` method returns the next value yielded by the generator, or raises `StopIteration` if the generator exits without yielding another value. When `send()` is called to start the generator, it must be called with `None` as the argument, because there is no `yield` expression that could receive the value.

`generator.`**`throw`**`(type[, value[, traceback]])`

Raises an exception of type `type` at the point where generator was paused, and returns the next value yielded by the generator function. If the generator exits without yielding another value, a `StopIteration` exception is raised. If the generator function does not catch the passed-in exception, or raises a different exception, then that exception propagates to the caller.

`generator.`**`close`**`()`

Raises a `GeneratorExit` at the point where the generator function was paused. If the generator function then raises `StopIteration` (by exiting normally, or due to already being closed) or `GeneratorExit` (by not catching the exception), close returns to its caller. If the generator yields a value, a `RuntimeError` is raised. If the generator raises any other exception, it is propagated to the caller. `close()` does nothing if the generator has already exited due to an exception or normal exit.

Here is a simple example that demonstrates the behavior of generators and generator functions:

```
>>> def echo(value=None):
...     print "Execution starts when 'next()' is called for the first time."
...     try:
...         while True:
...             try:
...                 value = (yield value)
...             except Exception, e:
...                 value = e
...     finally:
...         print "Don't forget to clean up when 'close()' is called."
...
>>> generator = echo(1)
>>> print generator.next()
Execution starts when 'next()' is called for the first time.
1
>>> print generator.next()
None
>>> print generator.send(2)
2
>>> generator.throw(TypeError, "spam")
TypeError('spam',)
>>> generator.close()
Don't forget to clean up when 'close()' is called.
```

See also:

PEP 0342 - Coroutines via Enhanced Generators The proposal to enhance the API and syntax of generators, making them usable as simple coroutines.

5.3 Primaries

Primaries represent the most tightly bound operations of the language. Their syntax is:

```
primary ::=  atom | attributeref | subscription | slicing | call
```

5.3.1 Attribute references

An attribute reference is a primary followed by a period and a name:

```
attributeref   ::=   primary "." identifier
```

The primary must evaluate to an object of a type that supports attribute references, e.g., a module, list, or an instance. This object is then asked to produce the attribute whose name is the identifier. If this attribute is not available, the exception AttributeError is raised. Otherwise, the type and value of the object produced is determined by the object. Multiple evaluations of the same attribute reference may yield different objects.

5.3.2 Subscriptions

A subscription selects an item of a sequence (string, tuple or list) or mapping (dictionary) object:

```
subscription   ::=   primary "[" expression_list "]"
```

The primary must evaluate to an object of a sequence or mapping type.

If the primary is a mapping, the expression list must evaluate to an object whose value is one of the keys of the mapping, and the subscription selects the value in the mapping that corresponds to that key. (The expression list is a tuple except if it has exactly one item.)

If the primary is a sequence, the expression (list) must evaluate to a plain integer. If this value is negative, the length of the sequence is added to it (so that, e.g., x[-1] selects the last item of x.) The resulting value must be a nonnegative integer less than the number of items in the sequence, and the subscription selects the item whose index is that value (counting from zero).

A string's items are characters. A character is not a separate data type but a string of exactly one character.

5.3.3 Slicings

A slicing selects a range of items in a sequence object (e.g., a string, tuple or list). Slicings may be used as expressions or as targets in assignment or del statements. The syntax for a slicing:

```
slicing            ::=   simple_slicing | extended_slicing
simple_slicing     ::=   primary "[" short_slice "]"
extended_slicing   ::=   primary "[" slice_list "]"
slice_list         ::=   slice_item ("," slice_item)* [","]
slice_item         ::=   expression | proper_slice | ellipsis
proper_slice       ::=   short_slice | long_slice
short_slice        ::=   [lower_bound] ":" [upper_bound]
long_slice         ::=   short_slice ":" [stride]
lower_bound        ::=   expression
upper_bound        ::=   expression
stride             ::=   expression
ellipsis           ::=   "..."
```

There is ambiguity in the formal syntax here: anything that looks like an expression list also looks like a slice list, so any subscription can be interpreted as a slicing. Rather than further complicating the syntax, this is disambiguated by defining that in this case the interpretation as a subscription takes priority over the interpretation as a slicing (this is the case if the slice list contains no proper slice nor ellipses). Similarly, when the slice list has exactly one short slice and no trailing comma, the interpretation as a simple slicing takes priority over that as an extended slicing.

The semantics for a simple slicing are as follows. The primary must evaluate to a sequence object. The lower and upper bound expressions, if present, must evaluate to plain integers; defaults are zero and the `sys.maxint`, respectively. If either bound is negative, the sequence's length is added to it. The slicing now selects all items with index *k* such that $i <= k < j$ where *i* and *j* are the specified lower and upper bounds. This may be an empty sequence. It is not an error if *i* or *j* lie outside the range of valid indexes (such items don't exist so they aren't selected).

The semantics for an extended slicing are as follows. The primary must evaluate to a mapping object, and it is indexed with a key that is constructed from the slice list, as follows. If the slice list contains at least one comma, the key is a tuple containing the conversion of the slice items; otherwise, the conversion of the lone slice item is the key. The conversion of a slice item that is an expression is that expression. The conversion of an ellipsis slice item is the built-in `Ellipsis` object. The conversion of a proper slice is a slice object (see section *The standard type hierarchy*) whose `start`, `stop` and `step` attributes are the values of the expressions given as lower bound, upper bound and stride, respectively, substituting `None` for missing expressions.

5.3.4 Calls

A call calls a callable object (e.g., a *function*) with a possibly empty series of *arguments*:

```
call                   ::=   primary "(" [argument_list [","]
                             | expression genexpr_for] ")"
argument_list          ::=   positional_arguments ["," keyword_arguments]
                             ["," "*" expression] ["," keyword_arguments]
                             ["," "**" expression]
                             | keyword_arguments ["," "*" expression]
                             ["," "**" expression]
                             | "*" expression ["," keyword_arguments] ["," "**" express
                             | "**" expression
positional_arguments   ::=   expression ("," expression)*
keyword_arguments      ::=   keyword_item ("," keyword_item)*
keyword_item           ::=   identifier "=" expression
```

A trailing comma may be present after the positional and keyword arguments but does not affect the semantics.

The primary must evaluate to a callable object (user-defined functions, built-in functions, methods of built-in objects, class objects, methods of class instances, and certain class instances themselves are callable; extensions may define additional callable object types). All argument expressions are evaluated before the call is attempted. Please refer to section *Function definitions* for the syntax of formal *parameter* lists.

If keyword arguments are present, they are first converted to positional arguments, as follows. First, a list of unfilled slots is created for the formal parameters. If there are N positional arguments, they are placed in the first N slots. Next, for each keyword argument, the identifier is used to determine the corresponding slot (if the identifier is the same as the first formal parameter name, the first slot is used, and so on). If the slot is already filled, a `TypeError` exception is raised. Otherwise, the value of the argument is placed in the slot, filling it (even if the expression is `None`, it fills the slot). When all arguments have been processed, the slots that are still unfilled are filled with the corresponding default value from the function definition. (Default values are calculated, once, when the function is defined; thus, a mutable object such as a list or dictionary used as default value will be shared by all calls that don't specify an argument value for the corresponding slot; this should usually be avoided.) If there are any unfilled slots for which no default value is specified, a `TypeError` exception is raised. Otherwise, the list of filled slots is used as the argument list for the call.

CPython implementation detail: An implementation may provide built-in functions whose positional parameters do not have names, even if they are 'named' for the purpose of documentation, and which therefore cannot be supplied by keyword. In CPython, this is the case for functions implemented in C that use `PyArg_ParseTuple()` to parse their arguments.

If there are more positional arguments than there are formal parameter slots, a `TypeError` exception is raised, unless a formal parameter using the syntax `*identifier` is present; in this case, that formal parameter receives a tuple containing the excess positional arguments (or an empty tuple if there were no excess positional arguments).

If any keyword argument does not correspond to a formal parameter name, a `TypeError` exception is raised, unless a formal parameter using the syntax `**identifier` is present; in this case, that formal parameter receives a dictionary containing the excess keyword arguments (using the keywords as keys and the argument values as corresponding values), or a (new) empty dictionary if there were no excess keyword arguments.

If the syntax `*expression` appears in the function call, `expression` must evaluate to an iterable. Elements from this iterable are treated as if they were additional positional arguments; if there are positional arguments $x1, ..., xN$, and `expression` evaluates to a sequence $y1, ..., yM$, this is equivalent to a call with M+N positional arguments $x1, ..., xN, y1, ..., yM$.

A consequence of this is that although the `*expression` syntax may appear *after* some keyword arguments, it is processed *before* the keyword arguments (and the `**expression` argument, if any – see below). So:

```
>>> def f(a, b):
...    print a, b
...
>>> f(b=1, *(2,))
2 1
>>> f(a=1, *(2,))
Traceback (most recent call last):
  File "<stdin>", line 1, in ?
TypeError: f() got multiple values for keyword argument 'a'
>>> f(1, *(2,))
1 2
```

It is unusual for both keyword arguments and the `*expression` syntax to be used in the same call, so in practice this confusion does not arise.

If the syntax `**expression` appears in the function call, `expression` must evaluate to a mapping, the contents of which are treated as additional keyword arguments. In the case of a keyword appearing in both `expression` and as an explicit keyword argument, a `TypeError` exception is raised.

Formal parameters using the syntax `*identifier` or `**identifier` cannot be used as positional argument slots or as keyword argument names. Formal parameters using the syntax `(sublist)` cannot be used as keyword argument names; the outermost sublist corresponds to a single unnamed argument slot, and the argument value is assigned to the sublist using the usual tuple assignment rules after all other parameter processing is done.

A call always returns some value, possibly `None`, unless it raises an exception. How this value is computed depends on the type of the callable object.

If it is—

a user-defined function: The code block for the function is executed, passing it the argument list. The first thing the code block will do is bind the formal parameters to the arguments; this is described in section *Function definitions*. When the code block executes a `return` statement, this specifies the return value of the function call.

a built-in function or method: The result is up to the interpreter; see *built-in-funcs* for the descriptions of built-in functions and methods.

a class object: A new instance of that class is returned.

a class instance method: The corresponding user-defined function is called, with an argument list that is one longer than the argument list of the call: the instance becomes the first argument.

a class instance: The class must define a `__call__()` method; the effect is then the same as if that method was called.

5.4 The power operator

The power operator binds more tightly than unary operators on its left; it binds less tightly than unary operators on its right. The syntax is:

```
power   ::=   primary ["**" u_expr]
```

Thus, in an unparenthesized sequence of power and unary operators, the operators are evaluated from right to left (this does not constrain the evaluation order for the operands): `-1**2` results in `-1`.

The power operator has the same semantics as the built-in `pow()` function, when called with two arguments: it yields its left argument raised to the power of its right argument. The numeric arguments are first converted to a common type. The result type is that of the arguments after coercion.

With mixed operand types, the coercion rules for binary arithmetic operators apply. For int and long int operands, the result has the same type as the operands (after coercion) unless the second argument is negative; in that case, all arguments are converted to float and a float result is delivered. For example, `10**2` returns `100`, but `10**-2` returns `0.01`. (This last feature was added in Python 2.2. In Python 2.1 and before, if both arguments were of integer types and the second argument was negative, an exception was raised).

Raising `0.0` to a negative power results in a `ZeroDivisionError`. Raising a negative number to a fractional power results in a `ValueError`.

5.5 Unary arithmetic and bitwise operations

All unary arithmetic and bitwise operations have the same priority:

```
u_expr   ::=   power | "-" u_expr | "+" u_expr | "~" u_expr
```

The unary - (minus) operator yields the negation of its numeric argument.

The unary + (plus) operator yields its numeric argument unchanged.

The unary ~ (invert) operator yields the bitwise inversion of its plain or long integer argument. The bitwise inversion of x is defined as `-(x+1)`. It only applies to integral numbers.

In all three cases, if the argument does not have the proper type, a `TypeError` exception is raised.

5.6 Binary arithmetic operations

The binary arithmetic operations have the conventional priority levels. Note that some of these operations also apply to certain non-numeric types. Apart from the power operator, there are only two levels, one for multiplicative operators and one for additive operators:

```
m_expr   ::=   u_expr | m_expr "*" u_expr | m_expr "//" u_expr | m_expr "/" u_expr
             | m_expr "%" u_expr
```

```
a_expr    ::=    m_expr | a_expr "+" m_expr | a_expr "-" m_expr
```

The * (multiplication) operator yields the product of its arguments. The arguments must either both be numbers, or one argument must be an integer (plain or long) and the other must be a sequence. In the former case, the numbers are converted to a common type and then multiplied together. In the latter case, sequence repetition is performed; a negative repetition factor yields an empty sequence.

The / (division) and // (floor division) operators yield the quotient of their arguments. The numeric arguments are first converted to a common type. Plain or long integer division yields an integer of the same type; the result is that of mathematical division with the 'floor' function applied to the result. Division by zero raises the ZeroDivisionError exception.

The % (modulo) operator yields the remainder from the division of the first argument by the second. The numeric arguments are first converted to a common type. A zero right argument raises the ZeroDivisionError exception. The arguments may be floating point numbers, e.g., 3.14%0.7 equals 0.34 (since 3.14 equals 4*0.7 + 0.34.) The modulo operator always yields a result with the same sign as its second operand (or zero); the absolute value of the result is strictly smaller than the absolute value of the second operand [2].

The integer division and modulo operators are connected by the following identity: x == (x/y)*y + (x%y). Integer division and modulo are also connected with the built-in function divmod(): divmod(x, y) == (x/y, x%y). These identities don't hold for floating point numbers; there similar identities hold approximately where x/y is replaced by floor(x/y) or floor(x/y) - 1 [3].

In addition to performing the modulo operation on numbers, the % operator is also overloaded by string and unicode objects to perform string formatting (also known as interpolation). The syntax for string formatting is described in the Python Library Reference, section *string-formatting*.

Deprecated since version 2.3: The floor division operator, the modulo operator, and the divmod() function are no longer defined for complex numbers. Instead, convert to a floating point number using the abs() function if appropriate.

The + (addition) operator yields the sum of its arguments. The arguments must either both be numbers or both sequences of the same type. In the former case, the numbers are converted to a common type and then added together. In the latter case, the sequences are concatenated.

The - (subtraction) operator yields the difference of its arguments. The numeric arguments are first converted to a common type.

5.7 Shifting operations

The shifting operations have lower priority than the arithmetic operations:

```
shift_expr    ::=    a_expr | shift_expr ( "<<" | ">>" ) a_expr
```

These operators accept plain or long integers as arguments. The arguments are converted to a common type. They shift the first argument to the left or right by the number of bits given by the second argument.

A right shift by *n* bits is defined as division by pow(2, n). A left shift by *n* bits is defined as multiplication with pow(2, n). Negative shift counts raise a ValueError exception.

---

[2] While abs(x%y) < abs(y) is true mathematically, for floats it may not be true numerically due to roundoff. For example, and assuming a platform on which a Python float is an IEEE 754 double-precision number, in order that -1e-100 % 1e100 have the same sign as 1e100, the computed result is -1e-100 + 1e100, which is numerically exactly equal to 1e100. The function math.fmod() returns a result whose sign matches the sign of the first argument instead, and so returns -1e-100 in this case. Which approach is more appropriate depends on the application.

[3] If x is very close to an exact integer multiple of y, it's possible for floor(x/y) to be one larger than (x-x%y)/y due to rounding. In such cases, Python returns the latter result, in order to preserve that divmod(x,y)[0] * y + x % y be very close to x.

Note: In the current implementation, the right-hand operand is required to be at most `sys.maxsize`. If the right-hand operand is larger than `sys.maxsize` an `OverflowError` exception is raised.

5.8 Binary bitwise operations

Each of the three bitwise operations has a different priority level:

```
and_expr  ::=  shift_expr | and_expr "&" shift_expr
xor_expr  ::=  and_expr | xor_expr "^" and_expr
or_expr   ::=  xor_expr | or_expr "|" xor_expr
```

The `&` operator yields the bitwise AND of its arguments, which must be plain or long integers. The arguments are converted to a common type.

The `^` operator yields the bitwise XOR (exclusive OR) of its arguments, which must be plain or long integers. The arguments are converted to a common type.

The `|` operator yields the bitwise (inclusive) OR of its arguments, which must be plain or long integers. The arguments are converted to a common type.

5.9 Comparisons

Unlike C, all comparison operations in Python have the same priority, which is lower than that of any arithmetic, shifting or bitwise operation. Also unlike C, expressions like `a < b < c` have the interpretation that is conventional in mathematics:

```
comparison    ::=  or_expr ( comp_operator or_expr )*
comp_operator ::=  "<" | ">" | "==" | ">=" | "<=" | "<>" | "!="
                 | "is" ["not"] | ["not"] "in"
```

Comparisons yield boolean values: `True` or `False`.

Comparisons can be chained arbitrarily, e.g., `x < y <= z` is equivalent to `x < y and y <= z`, except that `y` is evaluated only once (but in both cases `z` is not evaluated at all when `x < y` is found to be false).

Formally, if *a*, *b*, *c*, ..., *y*, *z* are expressions and *op1*, *op2*, ..., *opN* are comparison operators, then `a op1 b op2 c ... y opN z` is equivalent to `a op1 b and b op2 c and ... y opN z`, except that each expression is evaluated at most once.

Note that `a op1 b op2 c` doesn't imply any kind of comparison between *a* and *c*, so that, e.g., `x < y > z` is perfectly legal (though perhaps not pretty).

The forms `<>` and `!=` are equivalent; for consistency with C, `!=` is preferred; where `!=` is mentioned below `<>` is also accepted. The `<>` spelling is considered obsolescent.

The operators `<`, `>`, `==`, `>=`, `<=`, and `!=` compare the values of two objects. The objects need not have the same type. If both are numbers, they are converted to a common type. Otherwise, objects of different types *always* compare unequal, and are ordered consistently but arbitrarily. You can control comparison behavior of objects of non-built-in types by defining a `__cmp__` method or rich comparison methods like `__gt__`, described in section *Special method names*.

(This unusual definition of comparison was used to simplify the definition of operations like sorting and the `in` and `not in` operators. In the future, the comparison rules for objects of different types are likely to change.)

Comparison of objects of the same type depends on the type:

- Numbers are compared arithmetically.

- Strings are compared lexicographically using the numeric equivalents (the result of the built-in function `ord()`) of their characters. Unicode and 8-bit strings are fully interoperable in this behavior. [4]

- Tuples and lists are compared lexicographically using comparison of corresponding elements. This means that to compare equal, each element must compare equal and the two sequences must be of the same type and have the same length.

  If not equal, the sequences are ordered the same as their first differing elements. For example, `cmp([1,2,x],[1,2,y])` returns the same as `cmp(x,y)`. If the corresponding element does not exist, the shorter sequence is ordered first (for example, `[1,2] < [1,2,3]`).

- Mappings (dictionaries) compare equal if and only if their sorted (key, value) lists compare equal. [5] Outcomes other than equality are resolved consistently, but are not otherwise defined. [6]

- Most other objects of built-in types compare unequal unless they are the same object; the choice whether one object is considered smaller or larger than another one is made arbitrarily but consistently within one execution of a program.

The operators `in` and `not in` test for collection membership. `x in s` evaluates to true if x is a member of the collection s, and false otherwise. `x not in s` returns the negation of `x in s`. The collection membership test has traditionally been bound to sequences; an object is a member of a collection if the collection is a sequence and contains an element equal to that object. However, it make sense for many other object types to support membership tests without being a sequence. In particular, dictionaries (for keys) and sets support membership testing.

For the list and tuple types, `x in y` is true if and only if there exists an index i such that `x == y[i]` is true.

For the Unicode and string types, `x in y` is true if and only if x is a substring of y. An equivalent test is `y.find(x) != -1`. Note, x and y need not be the same type; consequently, `u'ab' in 'abc'` will return `True`. Empty strings are always considered to be a substring of any other string, so `"" in "abc"` will return `True`.

Changed in version 2.3: Previously, x was required to be a string of length 1.

For user-defined classes which define the `__contains__()` method, `x in y` is true if and only if `y.__contains__(x)` is true.

For user-defined classes which do not define `__contains__()` but do define `__iter__()`, `x in y` is true if some value z with `x == z` is produced while iterating over `y`. If an exception is raised during the iteration, it is as if `in` raised that exception.

Lastly, the old-style iteration protocol is tried: if a class defines `__getitem__()`, `x in y` is true if and only if there is a non-negative integer index i such that `x == y[i]`, and all lower integer indices do not raise `IndexError` exception. (If any other exception is raised, it is as if `in` raised that exception).

The operator `not in` is defined to have the inverse true value of `in`.

The operators `is` and `is not` test for object identity: `x is y` is true if and only if x and y are the same object. `x is not y` yields the inverse truth value. [7]

---

[4] While comparisons between unicode strings make sense at the byte level, they may be counter-intuitive to users. For example, the strings `u"\u00C7"` and `u"\u0043\u0327"` compare differently, even though they both represent the same unicode character (LATIN CAPITAL LETTER C WITH CEDILLA). To compare strings in a human recognizable way, compare using `unicodedata.normalize()`.

[5] The implementation computes this efficiently, without constructing lists or sorting.

[6] Earlier versions of Python used lexicographic comparison of the sorted (key, value) lists, but this was very expensive for the common case of comparing for equality. An even earlier version of Python compared dictionaries by identity only, but this caused surprises because people expected to be able to test a dictionary for emptiness by comparing it to `{}`.

[7] Due to automatic garbage-collection, free lists, and the dynamic nature of descriptors, you may notice seemingly unusual behaviour in certain uses of the `is` operator, like those involving comparisons between instance methods, or constants. Check their documentation for more info.

5.10 Boolean operations

```
or_test   ::=   and_test | or_test "or" and_test
and_test  ::=   not_test | and_test "and" not_test
not_test  ::=   comparison | "not" not_test
```

In the context of Boolean operations, and also when expressions are used by control flow statements, the following values are interpreted as false: False, None, numeric zero of all types, and empty strings and containers (including strings, tuples, lists, dictionaries, sets and frozensets). All other values are interpreted as true. (See the __nonzero__() special method for a way to change this.)

The operator not yields True if its argument is false, False otherwise.

The expression x and y first evaluates *x*; if *x* is false, its value is returned; otherwise, *y* is evaluated and the resulting value is returned.

The expression x or y first evaluates *x*; if *x* is true, its value is returned; otherwise, *y* is evaluated and the resulting value is returned.

(Note that neither and nor or restrict the value and type they return to False and True, but rather return the last evaluated argument. This is sometimes useful, e.g., if s is a string that should be replaced by a default value if it is empty, the expression s or 'foo' yields the desired value. Because not has to invent a value anyway, it does not bother to return a value of the same type as its argument, so e.g., not 'foo' yields False, not ''.)

5.11 Conditional Expressions

New in version 2.5.

```
conditional_expression   ::=   or_test ["if" or_test "else" expression]
expression               ::=   conditional_expression | lambda_expr
```

Conditional expressions (sometimes called a "ternary operator") have the lowest priority of all Python operations.

The expression x if C else y first evaluates the condition, *C* (*not x*); if *C* is true, *x* is evaluated and its value is returned; otherwise, *y* is evaluated and its value is returned.

See PEP 308 for more details about conditional expressions.

5.12 Lambdas

```
lambda_expr       ::=   "lambda" [parameter_list]: expression
old_lambda_expr   ::=   "lambda" [parameter_list]: old_expression
```

Lambda expressions (sometimes called lambda forms) have the same syntactic position as expressions. They are a shorthand to create anonymous functions; the expression lambda arguments: expression yields a function object. The unnamed object behaves like a function object defined with

```
def name(arguments):
    return expression
```

See section *Function definitions* for the syntax of parameter lists. Note that functions created with lambda expressions cannot contain statements.

5.13 Expression lists

```
expression_list ::= expression ( "," expression )* [","]
```

An expression list containing at least one comma yields a tuple. The length of the tuple is the number of expressions in the list. The expressions are evaluated from left to right.

The trailing comma is required only to create a single tuple (a.k.a. a *singleton*); it is optional in all other cases. A single expression without a trailing comma doesn't create a tuple, but rather yields the value of that expression. (To create an empty tuple, use an empty pair of parentheses: ().)

5.14 Evaluation order

Python evaluates expressions from left to right. Notice that while evaluating an assignment, the right-hand side is evaluated before the left-hand side.

In the following lines, expressions will be evaluated in the arithmetic order of their suffixes:

```
expr1, expr2, expr3, expr4
(expr1, expr2, expr3, expr4)
{expr1: expr2, expr3: expr4}
expr1 + expr2 * (expr3 - expr4)
expr1(expr2, expr3, *expr4, **expr5)
expr3, expr4 = expr1, expr2
```

5.15 Operator precedence

The following table summarizes the operator precedences in Python, from lowest precedence (least binding) to highest precedence (most binding). Operators in the same box have the same precedence. Unless the syntax is explicitly given, operators are binary. Operators in the same box group left to right (except for comparisons, including tests, which all have the same precedence and chain from left to right — see section *Comparisons* — and exponentiation, which groups from right to left).

Operator	Description
`lambda`	Lambda expression
`if - else`	Conditional expression
`or`	Boolean OR
`and`	Boolean AND
`not x`	Boolean NOT
`in`, `not in`, `is`, `is not`, `<`, `<=`, `>`, `>=`, `<>`, `!=`, `==`	Comparisons, including membership tests and identity tests
`|`	Bitwise OR
`^`	Bitwise XOR
`&`	Bitwise AND
`<<`, `>>`	Shifts
`+`, `-`	Addition and subtraction
`*`, `/`, `//`, `%`	Multiplication, division, remainder [8]
`+x`, `-x`, `~x`	Positive, negative, bitwise NOT
`**`	Exponentiation [9]
`x[index]`, `x[index:index]`, `x(arguments...)`, `x.attribute`	Subscription, slicing, call, attribute reference
`(expressions...)`, `[expressions...]`, `{key: value...}`, `` `expressions...` ``	Binding or tuple display, list display, dictionary display, string conversion

---

[8] The `%` operator is also used for string formatting; the same precedence applies.

[9] The power operator `**` binds less tightly than an arithmetic or bitwise unary operator on its right, that is, `2**-1` is `0.5`.

SIMPLE STATEMENTS

Simple statements are comprised within a single logical line. Several simple statements may occur on a single line separated by semicolons. The syntax for simple statements is:

```
simple_stmt   ::=   expression_stmt
                | assert_stmt
                | assignment_stmt
                | augmented_assignment_stmt
                | pass_stmt
                | del_stmt
                | print_stmt
                | return_stmt
                | yield_stmt
                | raise_stmt
                | break_stmt
                | continue_stmt
                | import_stmt
                | global_stmt
                | exec_stmt
```

6.1 Expression statements

Expression statements are used (mostly interactively) to compute and write a value, or (usually) to call a procedure (a function that returns no meaningful result; in Python, procedures return the value None). Other uses of expression statements are allowed and occasionally useful. The syntax for an expression statement is:

```
expression_stmt   ::=   expression_list
```

An expression statement evaluates the expression list (which may be a single expression).

In interactive mode, if the value is not None, it is converted to a string using the built-in repr() function and the resulting string is written to standard output (see section *The print statement*) on a line by itself. (Expression statements yielding None are not written, so that procedure calls do not cause any output.)

6.2 Assignment statements

Assignment statements are used to (re)bind names to values and to modify attributes or items of mutable objects:

```
assignment_stmt  ::=  (target_list "=")+ (expression_list | yield_expression)
target_list      ::=  target ("," target)* [","]
target           ::=  identifier
                   |  "(" target_list ")"
                   |  "[" target_list "]"
                   |  attributeref
                   |  subscription
                   |  slicing
```

(See section *Primaries* for the syntax definitions for the last three symbols.)

An assignment statement evaluates the expression list (remember that this can be a single expression or a comma-separated list, the latter yielding a tuple) and assigns the single resulting object to each of the target lists, from left to right.

Assignment is defined recursively depending on the form of the target (list). When a target is part of a mutable object (an attribute reference, subscription or slicing), the mutable object must ultimately perform the assignment and decide about its validity, and may raise an exception if the assignment is unacceptable. The rules observed by various types and the exceptions raised are given with the definition of the object types (see section *The standard type hierarchy*).

Assignment of an object to a target list is recursively defined as follows.

- If the target list is a single target: The object is assigned to that target.

- If the target list is a comma-separated list of targets: The object must be an iterable with the same number of items as there are targets in the target list, and the items are assigned, from left to right, to the corresponding targets.

Assignment of an object to a single target is recursively defined as follows.

- If the target is an identifier (name):

  - If the name does not occur in a `global` statement in the current code block: the name is bound to the object in the current local namespace.

  - Otherwise: the name is bound to the object in the current global namespace.

  The name is rebound if it was already bound. This may cause the reference count for the object previously bound to the name to reach zero, causing the object to be deallocated and its destructor (if it has one) to be called.

- If the target is a target list enclosed in parentheses or in square brackets: The object must be an iterable with the same number of items as there are targets in the target list, and its items are assigned, from left to right, to the corresponding targets.

- If the target is an attribute reference: The primary expression in the reference is evaluated. It should yield an object with assignable attributes; if this is not the case, `TypeError` is raised. That object is then asked to assign the assigned object to the given attribute; if it cannot perform the assignment, it raises an exception (usually but not necessarily `AttributeError`). Note: If the object is a class instance and the attribute reference occurs on both sides of the assignment operator, the RHS expression, `a.x` can access either an instance attribute or (if no instance attribute exists) a class attribute. The LHS target `a.x` is always set as an instance attribute, creating it if necessary. Thus, the two occurrences of `a.x` do not necessarily refer to the same attribute: if the RHS expression refers to a class attribute, the LHS creates a new instance attribute as the target of the assignment:

```
class Cls:
    x = 3               # class variable
```

```
inst = Cls()
inst.x = inst.x + 1   # writes inst.x as 4 leaving Cls.x as 3
```

This description does not necessarily apply to descriptor attributes, such as properties created with `property()`.

- If the target is a subscription: The primary expression in the reference is evaluated. It should yield either a mutable sequence object (such as a list) or a mapping object (such as a dictionary). Next, the subscript expression is evaluated.

  If the primary is a mutable sequence object (such as a list), the subscript must yield a plain integer. If it is negative, the sequence's length is added to it. The resulting value must be a nonnegative integer less than the sequence's length, and the sequence is asked to assign the assigned object to its item with that index. If the index is out of range, `IndexError` is raised (assignment to a subscripted sequence cannot add new items to a list).

  If the primary is a mapping object (such as a dictionary), the subscript must have a type compatible with the mapping's key type, and the mapping is then asked to create a key/datum pair which maps the subscript to the assigned object. This can either replace an existing key/value pair with the same key value, or insert a new key/value pair (if no key with the same value existed).

- If the target is a slicing: The primary expression in the reference is evaluated. It should yield a mutable sequence object (such as a list). The assigned object should be a sequence object of the same type. Next, the lower and upper bound expressions are evaluated, insofar they are present; defaults are zero and the sequence's length. The bounds should evaluate to (small) integers. If either bound is negative, the sequence's length is added to it. The resulting bounds are clipped to lie between zero and the sequence's length, inclusive. Finally, the sequence object is asked to replace the slice with the items of the assigned sequence. The length of the slice may be different from the length of the assigned sequence, thus changing the length of the target sequence, if the object allows it.

CPython implementation detail: In the current implementation, the syntax for targets is taken to be the same as for expressions, and invalid syntax is rejected during the code generation phase, causing less detailed error messages.

WARNING: Although the definition of assignment implies that overlaps between the left-hand side and the right-hand side are 'safe' (for example `a, b = b, a` swaps two variables), overlaps *within* the collection of assigned-to variables are not safe! For instance, the following program prints `[0, 2]`:

```
x = [0, 1]
i = 0
i, x[i] = 1, 2
print x
```

6.2.1 Augmented assignment statements

Augmented assignment is the combination, in a single statement, of a binary operation and an assignment statement:

```
augmented_assignment_stmt  ::=  augtarget augop (expression_list | yield_expression)
augtarget                  ::=  identifier | attributeref | subscription | slicing
augop                      ::=  "+=" | "-=" | "*=" | "/=" | "//=" | "%=" | "**="
                                | ">>=" | "<<=" | "&=" | "^=" | "|="
```

(See section *Primaries* for the syntax definitions for the last three symbols.)

An augmented assignment evaluates the target (which, unlike normal assignment statements, cannot be an unpacking) and the expression list, performs the binary operation specific to the type of assignment on the two operands, and assigns the result to the original target. The target is only evaluated once.

An augmented assignment expression like `x += 1` can be rewritten as `x = x + 1` to achieve a similar, but not exactly equal effect. In the augmented version, x is only evaluated once. Also, when possible, the actual operation is performed *in-place*, meaning that rather than creating a new object and assigning that to the target, the old object is modified instead.

With the exception of assigning to tuples and multiple targets in a single statement, the assignment done by augmented assignment statements is handled the same way as normal assignments. Similarly, with the exception of the possible *in-place* behavior, the binary operation performed by augmented assignment is the same as the normal binary operations.

For targets which are attribute references, the same *caveat about class and instance attributes* applies as for regular assignments.

6.3 The `assert` statement

Assert statements are a convenient way to insert debugging assertions into a program:

```
assert_stmt  ::=  "assert" expression ["," expression]
```

The simple form, `assert expression`, is equivalent to

```
if __debug__:
    if not expression: raise AssertionError
```

The extended form, `assert expression1, expression2`, is equivalent to

```
if __debug__:
    if not expression1: raise AssertionError(expression2)
```

These equivalences assume that `__debug__` and `AssertionError` refer to the built-in variables with those names. In the current implementation, the built-in variable `__debug__` is `True` under normal circumstances, `False` when optimization is requested (command line option -O). The current code generator emits no code for an assert statement when optimization is requested at compile time. Note that it is unnecessary to include the source code for the expression that failed in the error message; it will be displayed as part of the stack trace.

Assignments to `__debug__` are illegal. The value for the built-in variable is determined when the interpreter starts.

6.4 The `pass` statement

```
pass_stmt  ::=  "pass"
```

`pass` is a null operation — when it is executed, nothing happens. It is useful as a placeholder when a statement is required syntactically, but no code needs to be executed, for example:

```
def f(arg): pass    # a function that does nothing (yet)

class C: pass       # a class with no methods (yet)
```

6.5 The `del` statement

```
del_stmt  ::=  "del" target_list
```

Deletion is recursively defined very similar to the way assignment is defined. Rather than spelling it out in full details, here are some hints.

Deletion of a target list recursively deletes each target, from left to right.

Deletion of a name removes the binding of that name from the local or global namespace, depending on whether the name occurs in a global statement in the same code block. If the name is unbound, a NameError exception will be raised.

It is illegal to delete a name from the local namespace if it occurs as a free variable in a nested block.

Deletion of attribute references, subscriptions and slicings is passed to the primary object involved; deletion of a slicing is in general equivalent to assignment of an empty slice of the right type (but even this is determined by the sliced object).

6.6 The print statement

```
print_stmt   ::=   "print" ([expression ("," expression)* [","]]
                 | ">>" expression [("," expression)+ [","]])
```

print evaluates each expression in turn and writes the resulting object to standard output (see below). If an object is not a string, it is first converted to a string using the rules for string conversions. The (resulting or original) string is then written. A space is written before each object is (converted and) written, unless the output system believes it is positioned at the beginning of a line. This is the case (1) when no characters have yet been written to standard output, (2) when the last character written to standard output is a whitespace character except ' ', or (3) when the last write operation on standard output was not a print statement. (In some cases it may be functional to write an empty string to standard output for this reason.)

Note: Objects which act like file objects but which are not the built-in file objects often do not properly emulate this aspect of the file object's behavior, so it is best not to rely on this.

A ' \n' character is written at the end, unless the print statement ends with a comma. This is the only action if the statement contains just the keyword print.

Standard output is defined as the file object named stdout in the built-in module sys. If no such object exists, or if it does not have a write() method, a RuntimeError exception is raised.

print also has an extended form, defined by the second portion of the syntax described above. This form is sometimes referred to as "print chevron." In this form, the first expression after the >> must evaluate to a "file-like" object, specifically an object that has a write() method as described above. With this extended form, the subsequent expressions are printed to this file object. If the first expression evaluates to None, then sys.stdout is used as the file for output.

6.7 The return statement

```
return_stmt   ::=   "return" [expression_list]
```

return may only occur syntactically nested in a function definition, not within a nested class definition.

If an expression list is present, it is evaluated, else None is substituted.

return leaves the current function call with the expression list (or None) as return value.

When `return` passes control out of a `try` statement with a `finally` clause, that `finally` clause is executed before really leaving the function.

In a generator function, the `return` statement is not allowed to include an `expression_list`. In that context, a bare `return` indicates that the generator is done and will cause `StopIteration` to be raised.

6.8 The `yield` statement

```
yield_stmt    ::=    yield_expression
```

The `yield` statement is only used when defining a generator function, and is only used in the body of the generator function. Using a `yield` statement in a function definition is sufficient to cause that definition to create a generator function instead of a normal function.

When a generator function is called, it returns an iterator known as a generator iterator, or more commonly, a generator. The body of the generator function is executed by calling the generator's `next()` method repeatedly until it raises an exception.

When a `yield` statement is executed, the state of the generator is frozen and the value of `expression_list` is returned to `next()`'s caller. By "frozen" we mean that all local state is retained, including the current bindings of local variables, the instruction pointer, and the internal evaluation stack: enough information is saved so that the next time `next()` is invoked, the function can proceed exactly as if the `yield` statement were just another external call.

As of Python version 2.5, the `yield` statement is now allowed in the `try` clause of a `try ... finally` construct. If the generator is not resumed before it is finalized (by reaching a zero reference count or by being garbage collected), the generator-iterator's `close()` method will be called, allowing any pending `finally` clauses to execute.

For full details of `yield` semantics, refer to the *Yield expressions* section.

Note: In Python 2.2, the `yield` statement was only allowed when the `generators` feature has been enabled. This `__future__` import statement was used to enable the feature:

```
from __future__ import generators
```

See also:

PEP 0255 - Simple Generators The proposal for adding generators and the `yield` statement to Python.

PEP 0342 - Coroutines via Enhanced Generators The proposal that, among other generator enhancements, proposed allowing `yield` to appear inside a `try ... finally` block.

6.9 The `raise` statement

```
raise_stmt    ::=    "raise" [expression ["," expression ["," expression]]]
```

If no expressions are present, `raise` re-raises the last exception that was active in the current scope. If no exception is active in the current scope, a `TypeError` exception is raised indicating that this is an error (if running under IDLE, a `Queue.Empty` exception is raised instead).

Otherwise, `raise` evaluates the expressions to get three objects, using `None` as the value of omitted expressions. The first two objects are used to determine the *type* and *value* of the exception.

If the first object is an instance, the type of the exception is the class of the instance, the instance itself is the value, and the second object must be None.

If the first object is a class, it becomes the type of the exception. The second object is used to determine the exception value: If it is an instance of the class, the instance becomes the exception value. If the second object is a tuple, it is used as the argument list for the class constructor; if it is None, an empty argument list is used, and any other object is treated as a single argument to the constructor. The instance so created by calling the constructor is used as the exception value.

If a third object is present and not None, it must be a traceback object (see section *The standard type hierarchy*), and it is substituted instead of the current location as the place where the exception occurred. If the third object is present and not a traceback object or None, a TypeError exception is raised. The three-expression form of raise is useful to re-raise an exception transparently in an except clause, but raise with no expressions should be preferred if the exception to be re-raised was the most recently active exception in the current scope.

Additional information on exceptions can be found in section *Exceptions*, and information about handling exceptions is in section *The try statement*.

6.10 The break statement

```
break_stmt  ::=    "break"
```

break may only occur syntactically nested in a for or while loop, but not nested in a function or class definition within that loop.

It terminates the nearest enclosing loop, skipping the optional else clause if the loop has one.

If a for loop is terminated by break, the loop control target keeps its current value.

When break passes control out of a try statement with a finally clause, that finally clause is executed before really leaving the loop.

6.11 The continue statement

```
continue_stmt  ::=    "continue"
```

continue may only occur syntactically nested in a for or while loop, but not nested in a function or class definition or finally clause within that loop. It continues with the next cycle of the nearest enclosing loop.

When continue passes control out of a try statement with a finally clause, that finally clause is executed before really starting the next loop cycle.

6.12 The import statement

```
import_stmt       ::=    "import" module ["as" name] ( "," module ["as" name] )*
                         | "from" relative_module "import" identifier ["as" name]
                         ( "," identifier ["as" name] )*
                         | "from" relative_module "import" "(" identifier ["as" name]
                         ( "," identifier ["as" name] )* [","] ")"
```

```
                               | "from" module "import" "*"
module          ::=    (identifier ".")* identifier
relative_module ::=    "."* module | "."+
name            ::=    identifier
```

Import statements are executed in two steps: (1) find a module, and initialize it if necessary; (2) define a name or names in the local namespace (of the scope where the `import` statement occurs). The statement comes in two forms differing on whether it uses the `from` keyword. The first form (without `from`) repeats these steps for each identifier in the list. The form with `from` performs step (1) once, and then performs step (2) repeatedly.

To understand how step (1) occurs, one must first understand how Python handles hierarchical naming of modules. To help organize modules and provide a hierarchy in naming, Python has a concept of packages. A package can contain other packages and modules while modules cannot contain other modules or packages. From a file system perspective, packages are directories and modules are files.

Once the name of the module is known (unless otherwise specified, the term "module" will refer to both packages and modules), searching for the module or package can begin. The first place checked is `sys.modules`, the cache of all modules that have been imported previously. If the module is found there then it is used in step (2) of import.

If the module is not found in the cache, then `sys.meta_path` is searched (the specification for `sys.meta_path` can be found in **PEP 302**). The object is a list of *finder* objects which are queried in order as to whether they know how to load the module by calling their `find_module()` method with the name of the module. If the module happens to be contained within a package (as denoted by the existence of a dot in the name), then a second argument to `find_module()` is given as the value of the `__path__` attribute from the parent package (everything up to the last dot in the name of the module being imported). If a finder can find the module it returns a *loader* (discussed later) or returns `None`.

If none of the finders on `sys.meta_path` are able to find the module then some implicitly defined finders are queried. Implementations of Python vary in what implicit meta path finders are defined. The one they all do define, though, is one that handles `sys.path_hooks`, `sys.path_importer_cache`, and `sys.path`.

The implicit finder searches for the requested module in the "paths" specified in one of two places ("paths" do not have to be file system paths). If the module being imported is supposed to be contained within a package then the second argument passed to `find_module()`, `__path__` on the parent package, is used as the source of paths. If the module is not contained in a package then `sys.path` is used as the source of paths.

Once the source of paths is chosen it is iterated over to find a finder that can handle that path. The dict at `sys.path_importer_cache` caches finders for paths and is checked for a finder. If the path does not have a finder cached then `sys.path_hooks` is searched by calling each object in the list with a single argument of the path, returning a finder or raises `ImportError`. If a finder is returned then it is cached in `sys.path_importer_cache` and then used for that path entry. If no finder can be found but the path exists then a value of `None` is stored in `sys.path_importer_cache` to signify that an implicit, file-based finder that handles modules stored as individual files should be used for that path. If the path does not exist then a finder which always returns `None` is placed in the cache for the path.

If no finder can find the module then `ImportError` is raised. Otherwise some finder returned a loader whose `load_module()` method is called with the name of the module to load (see **PEP 302** for the original definition of loaders). A loader has several responsibilities to perform on a module it loads. First, if the module already exists in `sys.modules` (a possibility if the loader is called outside of the import machinery) then it is to use that module for initialization and not a new module. But if the module does not exist in `sys.modules` then it is to be added to that dict before initialization begins. If an error occurs during loading of the module and it was added to `sys.modules` it is to be removed from the dict. If an error occurs but the module was already in `sys.modules` it is left in the dict.

The loader must set several attributes on the module. `__name__` is to be set to the name of the module. `__file__` is to be the "path" to the file unless the module is built-in (and thus listed in `sys.builtin_module_names`) in which case the attribute is not set. If what is being imported is a package then `__path__` is to be set to a list of paths to be searched when looking for modules and packages contained within the package being imported. `__package__` is optional but should be set to the name of package that contains the module or package (the empty string is used for module not contained in a package). `__loader__` is also optional but should be set to the loader object that is loading the module.

If an error occurs during loading then the loader raises `ImportError` if some other exception is not already being propagated. Otherwise the loader returns the module that was loaded and initialized.

When step (1) finishes without raising an exception, step (2) can begin.

The first form of `import` statement binds the module name in the local namespace to the module object, and then goes on to import the next identifier, if any. If the module name is followed by `as`, the name following `as` is used as the local name for the module.

The `from` form does not bind the module name: it goes through the list of identifiers, looks each one of them up in the module found in step (1), and binds the name in the local namespace to the object thus found. As with the first form of `import`, an alternate local name can be supplied by specifying "`as` localname". If a name is not found, `ImportError` is raised. If the list of identifiers is replaced by a star ('`*`'), all public names defined in the module are bound in the local namespace of the `import` statement..

The *public names* defined by a module are determined by checking the module's namespace for a variable named `__all__`; if defined, it must be a sequence of strings which are names defined or imported by that module. The names given in `__all__` are all considered public and are required to exist. If `__all__` is not defined, the set of public names includes all names found in the module's namespace which do not begin with an underscore character ('`_`'). `__all__` should contain the entire public API. It is intended to avoid accidentally exporting items that are not part of the API (such as library modules which were imported and used within the module).

The `from` form with `*` may only occur in a module scope. If the wild card form of import — `import *` — is used in a function and the function contains or is a nested block with free variables, the compiler will raise a `SyntaxError`.

When specifying what module to import you do not have to specify the absolute name of the module. When a module or package is contained within another package it is possible to make a relative import within the same top package without having to mention the package name. By using leading dots in the specified module or package after `from` you can specify how high to traverse up the current package hierarchy without specifying exact names. One leading dot means the current package where the module making the import exists. Two dots means up one package level. Three dots is up two levels, etc. So if you execute `from . import mod` from a module in the `pkg` package then you will end up importing `pkg.mod`. If you execute `from ..subpkg2 import mod` from within `pkg.subpkg1` you will import `pkg.subpkg2.mod`. The specification for relative imports is contained within PEP 328.

`importlib.import_module()` is provided to support applications that determine which modules need to be loaded dynamically.

6.12.1 Future statements

A *future statement* is a directive to the compiler that a particular module should be compiled using syntax or semantics that will be available in a specified future release of Python. The future statement is intended to ease migration to future versions of Python that introduce incompatible changes to the language. It allows use of the new features on a per-module basis before the release in which the feature becomes standard.

```
future_statement  ::=   "from" "__future__" "import" feature ["as" name]
                        ("," feature ["as" name])*
                      | "from" "__future__" "import" "(" feature ["as" name]
                        ("," feature ["as" name])* [","] ")"
feature           ::=   identifier
name              ::=   identifier
```

A future statement must appear near the top of the module. The only lines that can appear before a future statement are:

- the module docstring (if any),

- comments,

- blank lines, and

- other future statements.

The features recognized by Python 2.6 are `unicode_literals`, `print_function`, `absolute_import`, `division`, `generators`, `nested_scopes` and `with_statement`. `generators`, `with_statement`, `nested_scopes` are redundant in Python version 2.6 and above because they are always enabled.

A future statement is recognized and treated specially at compile time: Changes to the semantics of core constructs are often implemented by generating different code. It may even be the case that a new feature introduces new incompatible syntax (such as a new reserved word), in which case the compiler may need to parse the module differently. Such decisions cannot be pushed off until runtime.

For any given release, the compiler knows which feature names have been defined, and raises a compile-time error if a future statement contains a feature not known to it.

The direct runtime semantics are the same as for any import statement: there is a standard module `__future__`, described later, and it will be imported in the usual way at the time the future statement is executed.

The interesting runtime semantics depend on the specific feature enabled by the future statement.

Note that there is nothing special about the statement:

```
import __future__ [as name]
```

That is not a future statement; it's an ordinary import statement with no special semantics or syntax restrictions.

Code compiled by an `exec` statement or calls to the built-in functions `compile()` and `execfile()` that occur in a module M containing a future statement will, by default, use the new syntax or semantics associated with the future statement. This can, starting with Python 2.2 be controlled by optional arguments to `compile()` — see the documentation of that function for details.

A future statement typed at an interactive interpreter prompt will take effect for the rest of the interpreter session. If an interpreter is started with the `-i` option, is passed a script name to execute, and the script includes a future statement, it will be in effect in the interactive session started after the script is executed.

See also:

PEP 236 - Back to the __future__ The original proposal for the __future__ mechanism.

6.13 The `global` statement

```
global_stmt  ::=  "global" identifier ("," identifier)*
```

The `global` statement is a declaration which holds for the entire current code block. It means that the listed identifiers are to be interpreted as globals. It would be impossible to assign to a global variable without `global`, although free variables may refer to globals without being declared global.

Names listed in a `global` statement must not be used in the same code block textually preceding that `global` statement.

Names listed in a `global` statement must not be defined as formal parameters or in a `for` loop control target, `class` definition, function definition, or `import` statement.

CPython implementation detail: The current implementation does not enforce the latter two restrictions, but programs should not abuse this freedom, as future implementations may enforce them or silently change the meaning of the program.

Programmer's note: the global is a directive to the parser. It applies only to code parsed at the same time as the global statement. In particular, a global statement contained in an exec statement does not affect the code block *containing* the exec statement, and code contained in an exec statement is unaffected by global statements in the code containing the exec statement. The same applies to the eval(), execfile() and compile() functions.

6.14 The exec statement

```
exec_stmt  ::=  "exec" or_expr ["in" expression ["," expression]]
```

This statement supports dynamic execution of Python code. The first expression should evaluate to either a Unicode string, a *Latin-1* encoded string, an open file object, a code object, or a tuple. If it is a string, the string is parsed as a suite of Python statements which is then executed (unless a syntax error occurs). [1] If it is an open file, the file is parsed until EOF and executed. If it is a code object, it is simply executed. For the interpretation of a tuple, see below. In all cases, the code that's executed is expected to be valid as file input (see section *File input*). Be aware that the return and yield statements may not be used outside of function definitions even within the context of code passed to the exec statement.

In all cases, if the optional parts are omitted, the code is executed in the current scope. If only the first expression after in is specified, it should be a dictionary, which will be used for both the global and the local variables. If two expressions are given, they are used for the global and local variables, respectively. If provided, *locals* can be any mapping object. Remember that at module level, globals and locals are the same dictionary. If two separate objects are given as *globals* and *locals*, the code will be executed as if it were embedded in a class definition.

The first expression may also be a tuple of length 2 or 3. In this case, the optional parts must be omitted. The form exec(expr, globals) is equivalent to exec expr in globals, while the form exec(expr, globals, locals) is equivalent to exec expr in globals, locals. The tuple form of exec provides compatibility with Python 3, where exec is a function rather than a statement.

Changed in version 2.4: Formerly, *locals* was required to be a dictionary.

As a side effect, an implementation may insert additional keys into the dictionaries given besides those corresponding to variable names set by the executed code. For example, the current implementation may add a reference to the dictionary of the built-in module __builtin__ under the key __builtins__ (!).

Programmer's hints: dynamic evaluation of expressions is supported by the built-in function eval(). The built-in functions globals() and locals() return the current global and local dictionary, respectively, which may be useful to pass around for use by exec.

---

[1] Note that the parser only accepts the Unix-style end of line convention. If you are reading the code from a file, make sure to use *universal newlines* mode to convert Windows or Mac-style newlines.

COMPOUND STATEMENTS

Compound statements contain (groups of) other statements; they affect or control the execution of those other statements in some way. In general, compound statements span multiple lines, although in simple incarnations a whole compound statement may be contained in one line.

The if, while and for statements implement traditional control flow constructs. try specifies exception handlers and/or cleanup code for a group of statements. Function and class definitions are also syntactically compound statements.

Compound statements consist of one or more 'clauses.' A clause consists of a header and a 'suite.' The clause headers of a particular compound statement are all at the same indentation level. Each clause header begins with a uniquely identifying keyword and ends with a colon. A suite is a group of statements controlled by a clause. A suite can be one or more semicolon-separated simple statements on the same line as the header, following the header's colon, or it can be one or more indented statements on subsequent lines. Only the latter form of suite can contain nested compound statements; the following is illegal, mostly because it wouldn't be clear to which if clause a following else clause would belong:

```
if test1: if test2: print x
```

Also note that the semicolon binds tighter than the colon in this context, so that in the following example, either all or none of the print statements are executed:

```
if x < y < z: print x; print y; print z
```

Summarizing:

```
compound_stmt   ::=   if_stmt
                      | while_stmt
                      | for_stmt
                      | try_stmt
                      | with_stmt
                      | funcdef
                      | classdef
                      | decorated
suite           ::=   stmt_list NEWLINE | NEWLINE INDENT statement+ DEDENT
statement       ::=   stmt_list NEWLINE | compound_stmt
stmt_list       ::=   simple_stmt (";" simple_stmt)* [";"]
```

Note that statements always end in a NEWLINE possibly followed by a DEDENT. Also note that optional continuation clauses always begin with a keyword that cannot start a statement, thus there are no ambiguities (the 'dangling else' problem is solved in Python by requiring nested if statements to be indented).

The formatting of the grammar rules in the following sections places each clause on a separate line for clarity.

7.1 The `if` statement

The `if` statement is used for conditional execution:

```
if_stmt   ::=    "if" expression ":"  suite
               ( "elif" expression ":"  suite )*
               ["else" ":"  suite]
```

It selects exactly one of the suites by evaluating the expressions one by one until one is found to be true (see section *Boolean operations* for the definition of true and false); then that suite is executed (and no other part of the `if` statement is executed or evaluated). If all expressions are false, the suite of the `else` clause, if present, is executed.

7.2 The `while` statement

The `while` statement is used for repeated execution as long as an expression is true:

```
while_stmt   ::=    "while" expression ":"  suite
                  ["else" ":"  suite]
```

This repeatedly tests the expression and, if it is true, executes the first suite; if the expression is false (which may be the first time it is tested) the suite of the `else` clause, if present, is executed and the loop terminates.

A `break` statement executed in the first suite terminates the loop without executing the `else` clause's suite. A `continue` statement executed in the first suite skips the rest of the suite and goes back to testing the expression.

7.3 The `for` statement

The `for` statement is used to iterate over the elements of a sequence (such as a string, tuple or list) or other iterable object:

```
for_stmt   ::=    "for" target_list "in" expression_list ":"  suite
                ["else" ":"  suite]
```

The expression list is evaluated once; it should yield an iterable object. An iterator is created for the result of the `expression_list`. The suite is then executed once for each item provided by the iterator, in the order of ascending indices. Each item in turn is assigned to the target list using the standard rules for assignments, and then the suite is executed. When the items are exhausted (which is immediately when the sequence is empty), the suite in the `else` clause, if present, is executed, and the loop terminates.

A `break` statement executed in the first suite terminates the loop without executing the `else` clause's suite. A `continue` statement executed in the first suite skips the rest of the suite and continues with the next item, or with the `else` clause if there was no next item.

The suite may assign to the variable(s) in the target list; this does not affect the next item assigned to it.

The target list is not deleted when the loop is finished, but if the sequence is empty, it will not have been assigned to at all by the loop. Hint: the built-in function `range()` returns a sequence of integers suitable to emulate the effect of Pascal's `for i := a to b do`; e.g., `range(3)` returns the list `[0, 1, 2]`.

Note: There is a subtlety when the sequence is being modified by the loop (this can only occur for mutable sequences, i.e. lists). An internal counter is used to keep track of which item is used next, and this is incremented on each iteration. When this counter has reached the length of the sequence the loop terminates. This means that if the suite deletes the current (or a previous) item from the sequence, the next item will be skipped (since it gets the index of the current item which has already been treated). Likewise, if the suite inserts an item in the sequence before the current item, the current item will be treated again the next time through the loop. This can lead to nasty bugs that can be avoided by making a temporary copy using a slice of the whole sequence, e.g.,

```
for x in a[:]:
    if x < 0: a.remove(x)
```

7.4 The `try` statement

The `try` statement specifies exception handlers and/or cleanup code for a group of statements:

```
try_stmt   ::=  try1_stmt | try2_stmt
try1_stmt  ::=  "try" ":"  suite
                ("except" [expression [("as" | ",") identifier]] ":"  suite)+
                ["else" ":"  suite]
                ["finally" ":"  suite]
try2_stmt  ::=  "try" ":"  suite
                "finally" ":"  suite
```

Changed in version 2.5: In previous versions of Python, `try...except...finally` did not work. `try...except` had to be nested in `try...finally`.

The `except` clause(s) specify one or more exception handlers. When no exception occurs in the `try` clause, no exception handler is executed. When an exception occurs in the `try` suite, a search for an exception handler is started. This search inspects the except clauses in turn until one is found that matches the exception. An expression-less except clause, if present, must be last; it matches any exception. For an except clause with an expression, that expression is evaluated, and the clause matches the exception if the resulting object is "compatible" with the exception. An object is compatible with an exception if it is the class or a base class of the exception object, or a tuple containing an item compatible with the exception.

If no except clause matches the exception, the search for an exception handler continues in the surrounding code and on the invocation stack. [1]

If the evaluation of an expression in the header of an except clause raises an exception, the original search for a handler is canceled and a search starts for the new exception in the surrounding code and on the call stack (it is treated as if the entire `try` statement raised the exception).

When a matching except clause is found, the exception is assigned to the target specified in that except clause, if present, and the except clause's suite is executed. All except clauses must have an executable block. When the end of this block is reached, execution continues normally after the entire try statement. (This means that if two nested handlers exist for the same exception, and the exception occurs in the try clause of the inner handler, the outer handler will not handle the exception.)

Before an except clause's suite is executed, details about the exception are assigned to three variables in the `sys` module: `sys.exc_type` receives the object identifying the exception; `sys.exc_value` receives the exception's parameter; `sys.exc_traceback` receives a traceback object (see section *The standard type hierarchy*) identifying the point in the program where the exception occurred. These details are also available through the `sys.exc_info()`

---

[1] The exception is propagated to the invocation stack unless there is a `finally` clause which happens to raise another exception. That new exception causes the old one to be lost.

function, which returns a tuple (exc_type, exc_value, exc_traceback). Use of the corresponding variables is deprecated in favor of this function, since their use is unsafe in a threaded program. As of Python 1.5, the variables are restored to their previous values (before the call) when returning from a function that handled an exception.

The optional else clause is executed if and when control flows off the end of the try clause. [2] Exceptions in the else clause are not handled by the preceding except clauses.

If finally is present, it specifies a 'cleanup' handler. The try clause is executed, including any except and else clauses. If an exception occurs in any of the clauses and is not handled, the exception is temporarily saved. The finally clause is executed. If there is a saved exception, it is re-raised at the end of the finally clause. If the finally clause raises another exception or executes a return or break statement, the saved exception is discarded:

```
>>> def f():
...     try:
...         1/0
...     finally:
...         return 42
...
>>> f()
42
```

The exception information is not available to the program during execution of the finally clause.

When a return, break or continue statement is executed in the try suite of a try...finally statement, the finally clause is also executed 'on the way out.' A continue statement is illegal in the finally clause. (The reason is a problem with the current implementation — this restriction may be lifted in the future).

The return value of a function is determined by the last return statement executed. Since the finally clause always executes, a return statement executed in the finally clause will always be the last one executed:

```
>>> def foo():
...     try:
...         return 'try'
...     finally:
...         return 'finally'
...
>>> foo()
'finally'
```

Additional information on exceptions can be found in section *Exceptions*, and information on using the raise statement to generate exceptions may be found in section *The raise statement*.

7.5 The with statement

New in version 2.5.

The with statement is used to wrap the execution of a block with methods defined by a context manager (see section *With Statement Context Managers*). This allows common try...except...finally usage patterns to be encapsulated for convenient reuse.

```
with_stmt ::=   "with" with_item ("," with_item)* ":"   suite
with_item ::=   expression ["as" target]
```

---

[2] Currently, control "flows off the end" except in the case of an exception or the execution of a return, continue, or break statement.

The execution of the `with` statement with one "item" proceeds as follows:

1. The context expression (the expression given in the `with_item`) is evaluated to obtain a context manager.

2. The context manager's `__exit__()` is loaded for later use.

3. The context manager's `__enter__()` method is invoked.

4. If a target was included in the `with` statement, the return value from `__enter__()` is assigned to it.

Note: The `with` statement guarantees that if the `__enter__()` method returns without an error, then `__exit__()` will always be called. Thus, if an error occurs during the assignment to the target list, it will be treated the same as an error occurring within the suite would be. See step 6 below.

---

5. The suite is executed.

6. The context manager's `__exit__()` method is invoked. If an exception caused the suite to be exited, its type, value, and traceback are passed as arguments to `__exit__()`. Otherwise, three `None` arguments are supplied.

   If the suite was exited due to an exception, and the return value from the `__exit__()` method was false, the exception is reraised. If the return value was true, the exception is suppressed, and execution continues with the statement following the `with` statement.

   If the suite was exited for any reason other than an exception, the return value from `__exit__()` is ignored, and execution proceeds at the normal location for the kind of exit that was taken.

With more than one item, the context managers are processed as if multiple `with` statements were nested:

```
with A() as a, B() as b:
    suite
```

is equivalent to

```
with A() as a:
    with B() as b:
        suite
```

Note: In Python 2.5, the `with` statement is only allowed when the `with_statement` feature has been enabled. It is always enabled in Python 2.6.

Changed in version 2.7: Support for multiple context expressions.

See also:

PEP 0343 - The "with" statement The specification, background, and examples for the Python `with` statement.

7.6 Function definitions

A function definition defines a user-defined function object (see section *The standard type hierarchy*):

```
decorated      ::=  decorators (classdef | funcdef)
decorators     ::=  decorator+
decorator      ::=  "@" dotted_name ["(" [argument_list [","]] ")"] NEWLINE
funcdef        ::=  "def" funcname "(" [parameter_list] ")" ":" suite
dotted_name    ::=  identifier ("." identifier)*
parameter_list ::=  (defparameter ",")*
                    ( "*" identifier ["," "**" identifier]
```

```
                       | "**" identifier
                       | defparameter [","] )
defparameter    ::=    parameter ["=" expression]
sublist         ::=    parameter ("," parameter)* [","]
parameter       ::=    identifier | "(" sublist ")"
funcname        ::=    identifier
```

A function definition is an executable statement. Its execution binds the function name in the current local namespace to a function object (a wrapper around the executable code for the function). This function object contains a reference to the current global namespace as the global namespace to be used when the function is called.

The function definition does not execute the function body; this gets executed only when the function is called. [3]

A function definition may be wrapped by one or more *decorator* expressions. Decorator expressions are evaluated when the function is defined, in the scope that contains the function definition. The result must be a callable, which is invoked with the function object as the only argument. The returned value is bound to the function name instead of the function object. Multiple decorators are applied in nested fashion. For example, the following code:

```
@f1(arg)
@f2
def func(): pass
```

is equivalent to:

```
def func(): pass
func = f1(arg)(f2(func))
```

When one or more top-level *parameters* have the form *parameter = expression*, the function is said to have "default parameter values." For a parameter with a default value, the corresponding *argument* may be omitted from a call, in which case the parameter's default value is substituted. If a parameter has a default value, all following parameters must also have a default value — this is a syntactic restriction that is not expressed by the grammar.

Default parameter values are evaluated when the function definition is executed. This means that the expression is evaluated once, when the function is defined, and that the same "pre-computed" value is used for each call. This is especially important to understand when a default parameter is a mutable object, such as a list or a dictionary: if the function modifies the object (e.g. by appending an item to a list), the default value is in effect modified. This is generally not what was intended. A way around this is to use None as the default, and explicitly test for it in the body of the function, e.g.:

```
def whats_on_the_telly(penguin=None):
    if penguin is None:
        penguin = []
    penguin.append("property of the zoo")
    return penguin
```

Function call semantics are described in more detail in section *Calls*. A function call always assigns values to all parameters mentioned in the parameter list, either from position arguments, from keyword arguments, or from default values. If the form "*identifier" is present, it is initialized to a tuple receiving any excess positional parameters, defaulting to the empty tuple. If the form "**identifier" is present, it is initialized to a new dictionary receiving any excess keyword arguments, defaulting to a new empty dictionary.

It is also possible to create anonymous functions (functions not bound to a name), for immediate use in expressions. This uses lambda expressions, described in section *Lambdas*. Note that the lambda expression is merely a shorthand for a simplified function definition; a function defined in a "def" statement can be passed around or assigned to another name just like a function defined by a lambda expression. The "def" form is actually more powerful since it allows the execution of multiple statements.

---

[3] A string literal appearing as the first statement in the function body is transformed into the function's __doc__ attribute and therefore the function's *docstring*.

Programmer's note: Functions are first-class objects. A "def" form executed inside a function definition defines a local function that can be returned or passed around. Free variables used in the nested function can access the local variables of the function containing the def. See section *Naming and binding* for details.

7.7 Class definitions

A class definition defines a class object (see section *The standard type hierarchy*):

```
classdef     ::=   "class" classname [inheritance] ":"  suite
inheritance  ::=   "(" [expression_list] ")"
classname    ::=   identifier
```

A class definition is an executable statement. It first evaluates the inheritance list, if present. Each item in the inheritance list should evaluate to a class object or class type which allows subclassing. The class's suite is then executed in a new execution frame (see section *Naming and binding*), using a newly created local namespace and the original global namespace. (Usually, the suite contains only function definitions.) When the class's suite finishes execution, its execution frame is discarded but its local namespace is saved. [4] A class object is then created using the inheritance list for the base classes and the saved local namespace for the attribute dictionary. The class name is bound to this class object in the original local namespace.

Programmer's note: Variables defined in the class definition are class variables; they are shared by all instances. To create instance variables, they can be set in a method with self.name = value. Both class and instance variables are accessible through the notation "self.name", and an instance variable hides a class variable with the same name when accessed in this way. Class variables can be used as defaults for instance variables, but using mutable values there can lead to unexpected results. For *new-style classes*, descriptors can be used to create instance variables with different implementation details.

Class definitions, like function definitions, may be wrapped by one or more *decorator* expressions. The evaluation rules for the decorator expressions are the same as for functions. The result must be a class object, which is then bound to the class name.

---

[4] A string literal appearing as the first statement in the class body is transformed into the namespace's __doc__ item and therefore the class's *docstring*.

TOP-LEVEL COMPONENTS

The Python interpreter can get its input from a number of sources: from a script passed to it as standard input or as program argument, typed in interactively, from a module source file, etc. This chapter gives the syntax used in these cases.

8.1 Complete Python programs

While a language specification need not prescribe how the language interpreter is invoked, it is useful to have a notion of a complete Python program. A complete Python program is executed in a minimally initialized environment: all built-in and standard modules are available, but none have been initialized, except for `sys` (various system services), `__builtin__` (built-in functions, exceptions and `None`) and `__main__`. The latter is used to provide the local and global namespace for execution of the complete program.

The syntax for a complete Python program is that for file input, described in the next section.

The interpreter may also be invoked in interactive mode; in this case, it does not read and execute a complete program but reads and executes one statement (possibly compound) at a time. The initial environment is identical to that of a complete program; each statement is executed in the namespace of `__main__`.

Under Unix, a complete program can be passed to the interpreter in three forms: with the *-c string* command line option, as a file passed as the first command line argument, or as standard input. If the file or standard input is a tty device, the interpreter enters interactive mode; otherwise, it executes the file as a complete program.

8.2 File input

All input read from non-interactive files has the same form:

```
file_input   ::=   (NEWLINE | statement)*
```

This syntax is used in the following situations:

- when parsing a complete Python program (from a file or from a string);
- when parsing a module;
- when parsing a string passed to the `exec` statement;

8.3 Interactive input

Input in interactive mode is parsed using the following grammar:

```
interactive_input  ::=  [stmt_list] NEWLINE | compound_stmt NEWLINE
```

Note that a (top-level) compound statement must be followed by a blank line in interactive mode; this is needed to help the parser detect the end of the input.

8.4 Expression input

There are two forms of expression input. Both ignore leading whitespace. The string argument to `eval()` must have the following form:

```
eval_input  ::=  expression_list NEWLINE*
```

The input line read by `input()` must have the following form:

```
input_input  ::=  expression_list NEWLINE
```

Note: to read 'raw' input line without interpretation, you can use the built-in function `raw_input()` or the `readline()` method of file objects.

FULL GRAMMAR SPECIFICATION

This is the full Python grammar, as it is read by the parser generator and used to parse Python source files:

```
# Grammar for Python

# Note:  Changing the grammar specified in this file will most likely
#        require corresponding changes in the parser module
#        (../Modules/parsermodule.c).  If you can't make the changes to
#        that module yourself, please co-ordinate the required changes
#        with someone who can; ask around on python-dev for help.  Fred
#        Drake <fdrake@acm.org> will probably be listening there.

# NOTE WELL: You should also follow all the steps listed in PEP 306,
# "How to Change Python's Grammar"

# Start symbols for the grammar:
#        single_input is a single interactive statement;
#        file_input is a module or sequence of commands read from an input file;
#        eval_input is the input for the eval() and input() functions.
# NB: compound_stmt in single_input is followed by extra NEWLINE!
single_input: NEWLINE | simple_stmt | compound_stmt NEWLINE
file_input: (NEWLINE | stmt)* ENDMARKER
eval_input: testlist NEWLINE* ENDMARKER

decorator: '@' dotted_name [ '(' [arglist] ')' ] NEWLINE
decorators: decorator+
decorated: decorators (classdef | funcdef)
funcdef: 'def' NAME parameters ':' suite
parameters: '(' [varargslist] ')'
varargslist: ((fpdef ['=' test] ',')*
               ('*' NAME [',' '**' NAME] | '**' NAME) |
               fpdef ['=' test] (',' fpdef ['=' test])* [','])
fpdef: NAME | '(' fplist ')'
fplist: fpdef (',' fpdef)* [',']

stmt: simple_stmt | compound_stmt
simple_stmt: small_stmt (';' small_stmt)* [';'] NEWLINE
small_stmt: (expr_stmt | print_stmt  | del_stmt | pass_stmt | flow_stmt |
             import_stmt | global_stmt | exec_stmt | assert_stmt)
expr_stmt: testlist (augassign (yield_expr|testlist) |
                    ('=' (yield_expr|testlist))*)
augassign: ('+=' | '-=' | '*=' | '/=' | '%=' | '&=' | '|=' | '^=' |
```

```
                    '<<=' | '>>=' | '**=' | '//=')
# For normal assignments, additional restrictions enforced by the interpreter
print_stmt: 'print' ( [ test (',' test)* [','] ] |
                      '>>' test [ (',' test)+ [','] ] )
del_stmt: 'del' exprlist
pass_stmt: 'pass'
flow_stmt: break_stmt | continue_stmt | return_stmt | raise_stmt | yield_stmt
break_stmt: 'break'
continue_stmt: 'continue'
return_stmt: 'return' [testlist]
yield_stmt: yield_expr
raise_stmt: 'raise' [test [',' test [',' test]]]
import_stmt: import_name | import_from
import_name: 'import' dotted_as_names
import_from: ('from' ('.'* dotted_name | '.'+)
              'import' ('*' | '(' import_as_names ')' | import_as_names))
import_as_name: NAME ['as' NAME]
dotted_as_name: dotted_name ['as' NAME]
import_as_names: import_as_name (',' import_as_name)* [',']
dotted_as_names: dotted_as_name (',' dotted_as_name)*
dotted_name: NAME ('.' NAME)*
global_stmt: 'global' NAME (',' NAME)*
exec_stmt: 'exec' expr ['in' test [',' test]]
assert_stmt: 'assert' test [',' test]

compound_stmt: if_stmt | while_stmt | for_stmt | try_stmt | with_stmt | funcdef | clas
if_stmt: 'if' test ':' suite ('elif' test ':' suite)* ['else' ':' suite]
while_stmt: 'while' test ':' suite ['else' ':' suite]
for_stmt: 'for' exprlist 'in' testlist ':' suite ['else' ':' suite]
try_stmt: ('try' ':' suite
           ((except_clause ':' suite)+
            ['else' ':' suite]
            ['finally' ':' suite] |
            'finally' ':' suite))
with_stmt: 'with' with_item (',' with_item)*  ':' suite
with_item: test ['as' expr]
# NB compile.c makes sure that the default except clause is last
except_clause: 'except' [test [('as' | ',') test]]
suite: simple_stmt | NEWLINE INDENT stmt+ DEDENT

# Backward compatibility cruft to support:
# [ x for x in lambda: True, lambda: False if x() ]
# even while also allowing:
# lambda x: 5 if x else 2
# (But not a mix of the two)
testlist_safe: old_test [(',' old_test)+ [',']]
old_test: or_test | old_lambdef
old_lambdef: 'lambda' [varargslist] ':' old_test

test: or_test ['if' or_test 'else' test] | lambdef
or_test: and_test ('or' and_test)*
and_test: not_test ('and' not_test)*
not_test: 'not' not_test | comparison
comparison: expr (comp_op expr)*
```

```
comp_op: '<'|'>'|'=='|'>='|'<='|'<>'|'!='|'in'|'not' 'in'|'is'|'is' 'not'
expr: xor_expr ('|' xor_expr)*
xor_expr: and_expr ('^' and_expr)*
and_expr: shift_expr ('&' shift_expr)*
shift_expr: arith_expr (('<<'|'>>') arith_expr)*
arith_expr: term (('+'|'-') term)*
term: factor (('*'|'/'|'%'|'//') factor)*
factor: ('+'|'-'|'~') factor | power
power: atom trailer* ['**' factor]
atom: ('(' [yield_expr|testlist_comp] ')' |
       '[' [listmaker] ']' |
       '{' [dictorsetmaker] '}' |
       '`' testlist1 '`' |
       NAME | NUMBER | STRING+)
listmaker: test ( list_for | (',' test)* [','] )
testlist_comp: test ( comp_for | (',' test)* [','] )
lambdef: 'lambda' [varargslist] ':' test
trailer: '(' [arglist] ')' | '[' subscriptlist ']' | '.' NAME
subscriptlist: subscript (',' subscript)* [',']
subscript: '.' '.' '.' | test | [test] ':' [test] [sliceop]
sliceop: ':' [test]
exprlist: expr (',' expr)* [',']
testlist: test (',' test)* [',']
dictorsetmaker: ( (test ':' test (comp_for | (',' test ':' test)* [','])) |
                  (test (comp_for | (',' test)* [','])) )

classdef: 'class' NAME ['(' [testlist] ')'] ':' suite

arglist: (argument ',')* (argument [',']
                         |'*' test (',' argument)* [',' '**' test]
                         |'**' test)
# The reason that keywords are test nodes instead of NAME is that using NAME
# results in an ambiguity. ast.c makes sure it's a NAME.
argument: test [comp_for] | test '=' test

list_iter: list_for | list_if
list_for: 'for' exprlist 'in' testlist_safe [list_iter]
list_if: 'if' old_test [list_iter]

comp_iter: comp_for | comp_if
comp_for: 'for' exprlist 'in' or_test [comp_iter]
comp_if: 'if' old_test [comp_iter]

testlist1: test (',' test)*

# not used in grammar, but may appear in "node" passed from Parser to Compiler
encoding_decl: NAME

yield_expr: 'yield' [testlist]
```

GLOSSARY

>>> The default Python prompt of the interactive shell. Often seen for code examples which can be executed interactively in the interpreter.

... The default Python prompt of the interactive shell when entering code for an indented code block or within a pair of matching left and right delimiters (parentheses, square brackets or curly braces).

2to3 A tool that tries to convert Python 2.x code to Python 3.x code by handling most of the incompatibilities which can be detected by parsing the source and traversing the parse tree.

2to3 is available in the standard library as lib2to3; a standalone entry point is provided as Tools/scripts/2to3. See *2to3-reference*.

abstract base class Abstract base classes complement *duck-typing* by providing a way to define interfaces when other techniques like hasattr() would be clumsy or subtly wrong (for example with *magic methods*). ABCs introduce virtual subclasses, which are classes that don't inherit from a class but are still recognized by isinstance() and issubclass(); see the abc module documentation. Python comes with many built-in ABCs for data structures (in the collections module), numbers (in the numbers module), and streams (in the io module). You can create your own ABCs with the abc module.

argument A value passed to a *function* (or *method*) when calling the function. There are two types of arguments:

- *keyword argument*: an argument preceded by an identifier (e.g. name=) in a function call or passed as a value in a dictionary preceded by **. For example, 3 and 5 are both keyword arguments in the following calls to complex():

```
complex(real=3, imag=5)
complex(**{'real': 3, 'imag': 5})
```

- *positional argument*: an argument that is not a keyword argument. Positional arguments can appear at the beginning of an argument list and/or be passed as elements of an *iterable* preceded by *. For example, 3 and 5 are both positional arguments in the following calls:

```
complex(3, 5)
complex(*(3, 5))
```

Arguments are assigned to the named local variables in a function body. See the *Calls* section for the rules governing this assignment. Syntactically, any expression can be used to represent an argument; the evaluated value is assigned to the local variable.

See also the *parameter* glossary entry and the FAQ question on *the difference between arguments and parameters*.

attribute A value associated with an object which is referenced by name using dotted expressions. For example, if an object *o* has an attribute *a* it would be referenced as *o.a*.

BDFL Benevolent Dictator For Life, a.k.a. Guido van Rossum, Python's creator.

bytes-like object An object that supports the *buffer protocol*, like `str`, `bytearray` or `memoryview`. Bytes-like objects can be used for various operations that expect binary data, such as compression, saving to a binary file or sending over a socket. Some operations need the binary data to be mutable, in which case not all bytes-like objects can apply.

bytecode Python source code is compiled into bytecode, the internal representation of a Python program in the CPython interpreter. The bytecode is also cached in `.pyc` and `.pyo` files so that executing the same file is faster the second time (recompilation from source to bytecode can be avoided). This "intermediate language" is said to run on a *virtual machine* that executes the machine code corresponding to each bytecode. Do note that bytecodes are not expected to work between different Python virtual machines, nor to be stable between Python releases.

A list of bytecode instructions can be found in the documentation for *the dis module*.

class A template for creating user-defined objects. Class definitions normally contain method definitions which operate on instances of the class.

classic class Any class which does not inherit from `object`. See *new-style class*. Classic classes have been removed in Python 3.

coercion The implicit conversion of an instance of one type to another during an operation which involves two arguments of the same type. For example, `int(3.15)` converts the floating point number to the integer 3, but in `3+4.5`, each argument is of a different type (one int, one float), and both must be converted to the same type before they can be added or it will raise a `TypeError`. Coercion between two operands can be performed with the `coerce` built-in function; thus, `3+4.5` is equivalent to calling `operator.add(*coerce(3, 4.5))` and results in `operator.add(3.0, 4.5)`. Without coercion, all arguments of even compatible types would have to be normalized to the same value by the programmer, e.g., `float(3)+4.5` rather than just `3+4.5`.

complex number An extension of the familiar real number system in which all numbers are expressed as a sum of a real part and an imaginary part. Imaginary numbers are real multiples of the imaginary unit (the square root of -1), often written i in mathematics or j in engineering. Python has built-in support for complex numbers, which are written with this latter notation; the imaginary part is written with a j suffix, e.g., `3+1j`. To get access to complex equivalents of the `math` module, use `cmath`. Use of complex numbers is a fairly advanced mathematical feature. If you're not aware of a need for them, it's almost certain you can safely ignore them.

context manager An object which controls the environment seen in a `with` statement by defining `__enter__()` and `__exit__()` methods. See **PEP 343**.

CPython The canonical implementation of the Python programming language, as distributed on python.org. The term "CPython" is used when necessary to distinguish this implementation from others such as Jython or IronPython.

decorator A function returning another function, usually applied as a function transformation using the `@wrapper` syntax. Common examples for decorators are `classmethod()` and `staticmethod()`.

The decorator syntax is merely syntactic sugar, the following two function definitions are semantically equivalent:

```
def f(...):
    ...
f = staticmethod(f)

@staticmethod
def f(...):
    ...
```

The same concept exists for classes, but is less commonly used there. See the documentation for *function definitions* and *class definitions* for more about decorators.

descriptor Any *new-style* object which defines the methods `__get__()`, `__set__()`, or `__delete__()`. When a class attribute is a descriptor, its special binding behavior is triggered upon attribute lookup. Normally, using *a.b* to get, set or delete an attribute looks up the object named *b* in the class dictionary for *a*, but if *b* is a descriptor, the respective descriptor method gets called. Understanding descriptors is a key to a deep understanding of Python because they are the basis for many features including functions, methods, properties, class methods, static methods, and reference to super classes.

For more information about descriptors' methods, see *Implementing Descriptors*.

dictionary An associative array, where arbitrary keys are mapped to values. The keys can be any object with `__hash__()` and `__eq__()` methods. Called a hash in Perl.

dictionary view The objects returned from `dict.viewkeys()`, `dict.viewvalues()`, and `dict.viewitems()` are called dictionary views. They provide a dynamic view on the dictionary's entries, which means that when the dictionary changes, the view reflects these changes. To force the dictionary view to become a full list use `list(dictview)`. See *dict-views*.

docstring A string literal which appears as the first expression in a class, function or module. While ignored when the suite is executed, it is recognized by the compiler and put into the `__doc__` attribute of the enclosing class, function or module. Since it is available via introspection, it is the canonical place for documentation of the object.

duck-typing A programming style which does not look at an object's type to determine if it has the right interface; instead, the method or attribute is simply called or used ("If it looks like a duck and quacks like a duck, it must be a duck.") By emphasizing interfaces rather than specific types, well-designed code improves its flexibility by allowing polymorphic substitution. Duck-typing avoids tests using `type()` or `isinstance()`. (Note, however, that duck-typing can be complemented with *abstract base classes*.) Instead, it typically employs `hasattr()` tests or *EAFP* programming.

EAFP Easier to ask for forgiveness than permission. This common Python coding style assumes the existence of valid keys or attributes and catches exceptions if the assumption proves false. This clean and fast style is characterized by the presence of many `try` and `except` statements. The technique contrasts with the *LBYL* style common to many other languages such as C.

expression A piece of syntax which can be evaluated to some value. In other words, an expression is an accumulation of expression elements like literals, names, attribute access, operators or function calls which all return a value. In contrast to many other languages, not all language constructs are expressions. There are also *statements* which cannot be used as expressions, such as `print` or `if`. Assignments are also statements, not expressions.

extension module A module written in C or C++, using Python's C API to interact with the core and with user code.

file object An object exposing a file-oriented API (with methods such as `read()` or `write()`) to an underlying resource. Depending on the way it was created, a file object can mediate access to a real on-disk file or to another type of storage or communication device (for example standard input/output, in-memory buffers, sockets, pipes, etc.). File objects are also called *file-like objects* or *streams*.

There are actually three categories of file objects: raw binary files, buffered binary files and text files. Their interfaces are defined in the `io` module. The canonical way to create a file object is by using the `open()` function.

file-like object A synonym for *file object*.

finder An object that tries to find the *loader* for a module. It must implement a method named `find_module()`. See **PEP 302** for details.

floor division Mathematical division that rounds down to nearest integer. The floor division operator is `//`. For example, the expression `11 // 4` evaluates to `2` in contrast to the `2.75` returned by float true division. Note that `(-11) // 4` is `-3` because that is `-2.75` rounded *downward*. See **PEP 238**.

function A series of statements which returns some value to a caller. It can also be passed zero or more *arguments* which may be used in the execution of the body. See also *parameter*, *method*, and the *Function definitions* section.

__future__ A pseudo-module which programmers can use to enable new language features which are not compatible with the current interpreter. For example, the expression `11/4` currently evaluates to `2`. If the module in which it is executed had enabled *true division* by executing:

```
from __future__ import division
```

the expression `11/4` would evaluate to `2.75`. By importing the `__future__` module and evaluating its variables, you can see when a new feature was first added to the language and when it will become the default:

```
>>> import __future__
>>> __future__.division
_Feature((2, 2, 0, 'alpha', 2), (3, 0, 0, 'alpha', 0), 8192)
```

garbage collection The process of freeing memory when it is not used anymore. Python performs garbage collection via reference counting and a cyclic garbage collector that is able to detect and break reference cycles.

generator A function which returns an iterator. It looks like a normal function except that it contains `yield` statements for producing a series of values usable in a for-loop or that can be retrieved one at a time with the `next()` function. Each `yield` temporarily suspends processing, remembering the location execution state (including local variables and pending try-statements). When the generator resumes, it picks-up where it left-off (in contrast to functions which start fresh on every invocation).

generator expression An expression that returns an iterator. It looks like a normal expression followed by a `for` expression defining a loop variable, range, and an optional `if` expression. The combined expression generates values for an enclosing function:

```
>>> sum(i*i for i in range(10))         # sum of squares 0, 1, 4, ... 81
285
```

GIL See *global interpreter lock*.

global interpreter lock The mechanism used by the *CPython* interpreter to assure that only one thread executes Python *bytecode* at a time. This simplifies the CPython implementation by making the object model (including critical built-in types such as `dict`) implicitly safe against concurrent access. Locking the entire interpreter makes it easier for the interpreter to be multi-threaded, at the expense of much of the parallelism afforded by multi-processor machines.

However, some extension modules, either standard or third-party, are designed so as to release the GIL when doing computationally-intensive tasks such as compression or hashing. Also, the GIL is always released when doing I/O.

Past efforts to create a "free-threaded" interpreter (one which locks shared data at a much finer granularity) have not been successful because performance suffered in the common single-processor case. It is believed that overcoming this performance issue would make the implementation much more complicated and therefore costlier to maintain.

hashable An object is *hashable* if it has a hash value which never changes during its lifetime (it needs a `__hash__()` method), and can be compared to other objects (it needs an `__eq__()` or `__cmp__()` method). Hashable objects which compare equal must have the same hash value.

Hashability makes an object usable as a dictionary key and a set member, because these data structures use the hash value internally.

All of Python's immutable built-in objects are hashable, while no mutable containers (such as lists or dictionaries) are. Objects which are instances of user-defined classes are hashable by default; they all compare unequal (except with themselves), and their hash value is their `id()`.

IDLE An Integrated Development Environment for Python. IDLE is a basic editor and interpreter environment which ships with the standard distribution of Python.

immutable An object with a fixed value. Immutable objects include numbers, strings and tuples. Such an object cannot be altered. A new object has to be created if a different value has to be stored. They play an important role in places where a constant hash value is needed, for example as a key in a dictionary.

integer division Mathematical division discarding any remainder. For example, the expression 11/4 currently evaluates to 2 in contrast to the 2.75 returned by float division. Also called *floor division*. When dividing two integers the outcome will always be another integer (having the floor function applied to it). However, if one of the operands is another numeric type (such as a float), the result will be coerced (see *coercion*) to a common type. For example, an integer divided by a float will result in a float value, possibly with a decimal fraction. Integer division can be forced by using the // operator instead of the / operator. See also *__future__*.

importing The process by which Python code in one module is made available to Python code in another module.

importer An object that both finds and loads a module; both a *finder* and *loader* object.

interactive Python has an interactive interpreter which means you can enter statements and expressions at the interpreter prompt, immediately execute them and see their results. Just launch python with no arguments (possibly by selecting it from your computer's main menu). It is a very powerful way to test out new ideas or inspect modules and packages (remember help(x)).

interpreted Python is an interpreted language, as opposed to a compiled one, though the distinction can be blurry because of the presence of the bytecode compiler. This means that source files can be run directly without explicitly creating an executable which is then run. Interpreted languages typically have a shorter development/debug cycle than compiled ones, though their programs generally also run more slowly. See also *interactive*.

iterable An object capable of returning its members one at a time. Examples of iterables include all sequence types (such as list, str, and tuple) and some non-sequence types like dict and file and objects of any classes you define with an __iter__() or __getitem__() method. Iterables can be used in a for loop and in many other places where a sequence is needed (zip(), map(), ...). When an iterable object is passed as an argument to the built-in function iter(), it returns an iterator for the object. This iterator is good for one pass over the set of values. When using iterables, it is usually not necessary to call iter() or deal with iterator objects yourself. The for statement does that automatically for you, creating a temporary unnamed variable to hold the iterator for the duration of the loop. See also *iterator*, *sequence*, and *generator*.

iterator An object representing a stream of data. Repeated calls to the iterator's next() method return successive items in the stream. When no more data are available a StopIteration exception is raised instead. At this point, the iterator object is exhausted and any further calls to its next() method just raise StopIteration again. Iterators are required to have an __iter__() method that returns the iterator object itself so every iterator is also iterable and may be used in most places where other iterables are accepted. One notable exception is code which attempts multiple iteration passes. A container object (such as a list) produces a fresh new iterator each time you pass it to the iter() function or use it in a for loop. Attempting this with an iterator will just return the same exhausted iterator object used in the previous iteration pass, making it appear like an empty container.

More information can be found in *typeiter*.

key function A key function or collation function is a callable that returns a value used for sorting or ordering. For example, locale.strxfrm() is used to produce a sort key that is aware of locale specific sort conventions.

A number of tools in Python accept key functions to control how elements are ordered or grouped. They include min(), max(), sorted(), list.sort(), heapq.nsmallest(), heapq.nlargest(), and itertools.groupby().

There are several ways to create a key function. For example. the str.lower() method can serve as a key function for case insensitive sorts. Alternatively, an ad-hoc key function can be built from a lambda expression such as lambda r: (r[0], r[2]). Also, the operator module provides three key function constructors: attrgetter(), itemgetter(), and methodcaller(). See the *Sorting HOW TO* for examples of how to create and use key functions.

keyword argument See *argument*.

lambda   An anonymous inline function consisting of a single *expression* which is evaluated when the function is called. The syntax to create a lambda function is `lambda [arguments]: expression`

LBYL   Look before you leap. This coding style explicitly tests for pre-conditions before making calls or lookups. This style contrasts with the *EAFP* approach and is characterized by the presence of many `if` statements.

In a multi-threaded environment, the LBYL approach can risk introducing a race condition between "the looking" and "the leaping". For example, the code, `if key in mapping: return mapping[key]` can fail if another thread removes *key* from *mapping* after the test, but before the lookup. This issue can be solved with locks or by using the EAFP approach.

list   A built-in Python *sequence*. Despite its name it is more akin to an array in other languages than to a linked list since access to elements are O(1).

list comprehension   A compact way to process all or part of the elements in a sequence and return a list with the results. `result = ["0x%02x" % x for x in range(256) if x % 2 == 0]` generates a list of strings containing even hex numbers (0x..) in the range from 0 to 255. The `if` clause is optional. If omitted, all elements in `range(256)` are processed.

loader   An object that loads a module. It must define a method named `load_module()`. A loader is typically returned by a *finder*. See **PEP 302** for details.

mapping   A container object that supports arbitrary key lookups and implements the methods specified in the `Mapping` or `MutableMapping` *abstract base classes*. Examples include `dict`, `collections.defaultdict`, `collections.OrderedDict` and `collections.Counter`.

metaclass   The class of a class. Class definitions create a class name, a class dictionary, and a list of base classes. The metaclass is responsible for taking those three arguments and creating the class. Most object oriented programming languages provide a default implementation. What makes Python special is that it is possible to create custom metaclasses. Most users never need this tool, but when the need arises, metaclasses can provide powerful, elegant solutions. They have been used for logging attribute access, adding thread-safety, tracking object creation, implementing singletons, and many other tasks.

More information can be found in *Customizing class creation*.

method   A function which is defined inside a class body. If called as an attribute of an instance of that class, the method will get the instance object as its first *argument* (which is usually called `self`). See *function* and *nested scope*.

method resolution order   Method Resolution Order is the order in which base classes are searched for a member during lookup. See *The Python 2.3 Method Resolution Order*.

module   An object that serves as an organizational unit of Python code. Modules have a namespace containing arbitrary Python objects. Modules are loaded into Python by the process of *importing*.

See also *package*.

MRO   See *method resolution order*.

mutable   Mutable objects can change their value but keep their `id()`. See also *immutable*.

named tuple   Any tuple-like class whose indexable elements are also accessible using named attributes (for example, `time.localtime()` returns a tuple-like object where the *year* is accessible either with an index such as `t[0]` or with a named attribute like `t.tm_year`).

A named tuple can be a built-in type such as `time.struct_time`, or it can be created with a regular class definition. A full featured named tuple can also be created with the factory function `collections.namedtuple()`. The latter approach automatically provides extra features such as a self-documenting representation like `Employee(name='jones', title='programmer')`.

namespace   The place where a variable is stored. Namespaces are implemented as dictionaries. There are the local, global and built-in namespaces as well as nested namespaces in objects (in methods). Namespaces support modularity by preventing naming conflicts. For instance, the functions `__builtin__.open()` and `os.open()` are distinguished by their namespaces. Namespaces also aid readability and maintainability by making it clear which module implements a function. For instance, writing `random.seed()` or `itertools.izip()` makes it clear that those functions are implemented by the `random` and `itertools` modules, respectively.

nested scope The ability to refer to a variable in an enclosing definition. For instance, a function defined inside another function can refer to variables in the outer function. Note that nested scopes work only for reference and not for assignment which will always write to the innermost scope. In contrast, local variables both read and write in the innermost scope. Likewise, global variables read and write to the global namespace.

new-style class Any class which inherits from `object`. This includes all built-in types like `list` and `dict`. Only new-style classes can use Python's newer, versatile features like `__slots__`, descriptors, properties, and `__getattribute__()`.

More information can be found in *New-style and classic classes*.

object Any data with state (attributes or value) and defined behavior (methods). Also the ultimate base class of any *new-style class*.

package A Python *module* which can contain submodules or recursively, subpackages. Technically, a package is a Python module with an `__path__` attribute.

parameter A named entity in a *function* (or method) definition that specifies an *argument* (or in some cases, arguments) that the function can accept. There are four types of parameters:

- *positional-or-keyword*: specifies an argument that can be passed either *positionally* or as a *keyword argument*. This is the default kind of parameter, for example *foo* and *bar* in the following:

  ```
  def func(foo, bar=None): ...
  ```

- *positional-only*: specifies an argument that can be supplied only by position. Python has no syntax for defining positional-only parameters. However, some built-in functions have positional-only parameters (e.g. `abs()`).

- *var-positional*: specifies that an arbitrary sequence of positional arguments can be provided (in addition to any positional arguments already accepted by other parameters). Such a parameter can be defined by prepending the parameter name with `*`, for example *args* in the following:

  ```
  def func(*args, **kwargs): ...
  ```

- *var-keyword*: specifies that arbitrarily many keyword arguments can be provided (in addition to any keyword arguments already accepted by other parameters). Such a parameter can be defined by prepending the parameter name with `**`, for example *kwargs* in the example above.

Parameters can specify both optional and required arguments, as well as default values for some optional arguments.

See also the *argument* glossary entry, the FAQ question on *the difference between arguments and parameters*, and the *Function definitions* section.

positional argument See *argument*.

Python 3000 Nickname for the Python 3.x release line (coined long ago when the release of version 3 was something in the distant future.) This is also abbreviated "Py3k".

Pythonic An idea or piece of code which closely follows the most common idioms of the Python language, rather than implementing code using concepts common to other languages. For example, a common idiom in Python is to loop over all elements of an iterable using a `for` statement. Many other languages don't have this type of construct, so people unfamiliar with Python sometimes use a numerical counter instead:

```
for i in range(len(food)):
    print food[i]
```

As opposed to the cleaner, Pythonic method:

```
for piece in food:
    print piece
```

reference count The number of references to an object. When the reference count of an object drops to zero, it is deallocated. Reference counting is generally not visible to Python code, but it is a key element of the *CPython* implementation. The `sys` module defines a `getrefcount()` function that programmers can call to return the reference count for a particular object.

__slots__ A declaration inside a *new-style class* that saves memory by pre-declaring space for instance attributes and eliminating instance dictionaries. Though popular, the technique is somewhat tricky to get right and is best reserved for rare cases where there are large numbers of instances in a memory-critical application.

sequence An *iterable* which supports efficient element access using integer indices via the `__getitem__()` special method and defines a `len()` method that returns the length of the sequence. Some built-in sequence types are `list`, `str`, `tuple`, and `unicode`. Note that `dict` also supports `__getitem__()` and `__len__()`, but is considered a mapping rather than a sequence because the lookups use arbitrary *immutable* keys rather than integers.

slice An object usually containing a portion of a *sequence*. A slice is created using the subscript notation, `[]` with colons between numbers when several are given, such as in `variable_name[1:3:5]`. The bracket (subscript) notation uses `slice` objects internally (or in older versions, `__getslice__()` and `__setslice__()`).

special method A method that is called implicitly by Python to execute a certain operation on a type, such as addition. Such methods have names starting and ending with double underscores. Special methods are documented in *Special method names*.

statement A statement is part of a suite (a "block" of code). A statement is either an *expression* or one of several constructs with a keyword, such as `if`, `while` or `for`.

struct sequence A tuple with named elements. Struct sequences expose an interface similiar to *named tuple* in that elements can either be accessed either by index or as an attribute. However, they do not have any of the named tuple methods like `_make()` or `_asdict()`. Examples of struct sequences include `sys.float_info` and the return value of `os.stat()`.

triple-quoted string A string which is bound by three instances of either a quotation mark (") or an apostrophe ('). While they don't provide any functionality not available with single-quoted strings, they are useful for a number of reasons. They allow you to include unescaped single and double quotes within a string and they can span multiple lines without the use of the continuation character, making them especially useful when writing docstrings.

type The type of a Python object determines what kind of object it is; every object has a type. An object's type is accessible as its `__class__` attribute or can be retrieved with `type(obj)`.

universal newlines A manner of interpreting text streams in which all of the following are recognized as ending a line: the Unix end-of-line convention `'\n'`, the Windows convention `'\r\n'`, and the old Macintosh convention `'\r'`. See PEP 278 and PEP 3116, as well as `str.splitlines()` for an additional use.

virtual environment A cooperatively isolated runtime environment that allows Python users and applications to install and upgrade Python distribution packages without interfering with the behaviour of other Python applications running on the same system.

virtual machine A computer defined entirely in software. Python's virtual machine executes the *bytecode* emitted by the bytecode compiler.

Zen of Python Listing of Python design principles and philosophies that are helpful in understanding and using the language. The listing can be found by typing "`import this`" at the interactive prompt.

ABOUT THESE DOCUMENTS

These documents are generated from reStructuredText sources by Sphinx, a document processor specifically written for the Python documentation.

Development of the documentation and its toolchain is an entirely volunteer effort, just like Python itself. If you want to contribute, please take a look at the *reporting-bugs* page for information on how to do so. New volunteers are always welcome!

Many thanks go to:

- Fred L. Drake, Jr., the creator of the original Python documentation toolset and writer of much of the content;

- the Docutils project for creating reStructuredText and the Docutils suite;

- Fredrik Lundh for his Alternative Python Reference project from which Sphinx got many good ideas.

B.1 Contributors to the Python Documentation

Many people have contributed to the Python language, the Python standard library, and the Python documentation. See Misc/ACKS in the Python source distribution for a partial list of contributors.

It is only with the input and contributions of the Python community that Python has such wonderful documentation – Thank You!

HISTORY AND LICENSE

C.1 History of the software

Python was created in the early 1990s by Guido van Rossum at Stichting Mathematisch Centrum (CWI, see http://www.cwi.nl/) in the Netherlands as a successor of a language called ABC. Guido remains Python's principal author, although it includes many contributions from others.

In 1995, Guido continued his work on Python at the Corporation for National Research Initiatives (CNRI, see http://www.cnri.reston.va.us/) in Reston, Virginia where he released several versions of the software.

In May 2000, Guido and the Python core development team moved to BeOpen.com to form the BeOpen Python-Labs team. In October of the same year, the PythonLabs team moved to Digital Creations (now Zope Corporation; see http://www.zope.com/). In 2001, the Python Software Foundation (PSF, see https://www.python.org/psf/) was formed, a non-profit organization created specifically to own Python-related Intellectual Property. Zope Corporation is a sponsoring member of the PSF.

All Python releases are Open Source (see http://opensource.org/ for the Open Source Definition). Historically, most, but not all, Python releases have also been GPL-compatible; the table below summarizes the various releases.

Release	Derived from	Year	Owner	GPL compatible?
0.9.0 thru 1.2	n/a	1991-1995	CWI	yes
1.3 thru 1.5.2	1.2	1995-1999	CNRI	yes
1.6	1.5.2	2000	CNRI	no
2.0	1.6	2000	BeOpen.com	no
1.6.1	1.6	2001	CNRI	no
2.1	2.0+1.6.1	2001	PSF	no
2.0.1	2.0+1.6.1	2001	PSF	yes
2.1.1	2.1+2.0.1	2001	PSF	yes
2.1.2	2.1.1	2002	PSF	yes
2.1.3	2.1.2	2002	PSF	yes
2.2 and above	2.1.1	2001-now	PSF	yes

Note: GPL-compatible doesn't mean that we're distributing Python under the GPL. All Python licenses, unlike the GPL, let you distribute a modified version without making your changes open source. The GPL-compatible licenses make it possible to combine Python with other software that is released under the GPL; the others don't.

Thanks to the many outside volunteers who have worked under Guido's direction to make these releases possible.

C.2 Terms and conditions for accessing or otherwise using Python

PSF LICENSE AGREEMENT FOR PYTHON 2.7.10

1. This LICENSE AGREEMENT is between the Python Software Foundation ("PSF"), and the Individual or Organization ("Licensee") accessing and otherwise using Python 2.7.10 software in source or binary form and its associated documentation.

2. Subject to the terms and conditions of this License Agreement, PSF hereby grants Licensee a nonexclusive, royalty-free, world-wide license to reproduce, analyze, test, perform and/or display publicly, prepare derivative works, distribute, and otherwise use Python 2.7.10 alone or in any derivative version, provided, however, that PSF's License Agreement and PSF's notice of copyright, i.e., "Copyright © 2001-2015 Python Software Foundation; All Rights Reserved" are retained in Python 2.7.10 alone or in any derivative version prepared by Licensee.

3. In the event Licensee prepares a derivative work that is based on or incorporates Python 2.7.10 or any part thereof, and wants to make the derivative work available to others as provided herein, then Licensee hereby agrees to include in any such work a brief summary of the changes made to Python 2.7.10.

4. PSF is making Python 2.7.10 available to Licensee on an "AS IS" basis. PSF MAKES NO REPRESENTATIONS OR WARRANTIES, EXPRESS OR IMPLIED. BY WAY OF EXAMPLE, BUT NOT LIMITATION, PSF MAKES NO AND DISCLAIMS ANY REPRESENTATION OR WARRANTY OF MERCHANTABILITY OR FITNESS FOR ANY PARTICULAR PURPOSE OR THAT THE USE OF PYTHON 2.7.10 WILL NOT INFRINGE ANY THIRD PARTY RIGHTS.

5. PSF SHALL NOT BE LIABLE TO LICENSEE OR ANY OTHER USERS OF PYTHON 2.7.10 FOR ANY INCIDENTAL, SPECIAL, OR CONSEQUENTIAL DAMAGES OR LOSS AS A RESULT OF MODIFYING, DISTRIBUTING, OR OTHERWISE USING PYTHON 2.7.10, OR ANY DERIVATIVE THEREOF, EVEN IF ADVISED OF THE POSSIBILITY THEREOF.

6. This License Agreement will automatically terminate upon a material breach of its terms and conditions.

7. Nothing in this License Agreement shall be deemed to create any relationship of agency, partnership, or joint venture between PSF and Licensee. This License Agreement does not grant permission to use PSF trademarks or trade name in a trademark sense to endorse or promote products or services of Licensee, or any third party.

8. By copying, installing or otherwise using Python 2.7.10, Licensee agrees to be bound by the terms and conditions of this License Agreement.

BEOPEN.COM LICENSE AGREEMENT FOR PYTHON 2.0

BEOPEN PYTHON OPEN SOURCE LICENSE AGREEMENT VERSION 1

1. This LICENSE AGREEMENT is between BeOpen.com ("BeOpen"), having an office at 160 Saratoga Avenue, Santa Clara, CA 95051, and the Individual or Organization ("Licensee") accessing and otherwise using this software in source or binary form and its associated documentation ("the Software").

2. Subject to the terms and conditions of this BeOpen Python License Agreement, BeOpen hereby grants Licensee a non-exclusive, royalty-free, world-wide license to reproduce, analyze, test, perform and/or display publicly, prepare derivative works, distribute, and otherwise use the Software alone or in any derivative version, provided, however, that the BeOpen Python License is retained in the Software, alone or in any derivative version prepared by Licensee.

3. BeOpen is making the Software available to Licensee on an "AS IS" basis. BEOPEN MAKES NO REPRESENTATIONS OR WARRANTIES, EXPRESS OR IMPLIED. BY WAY OF EXAMPLE, BUT NOT LIMITATION, BEOPEN MAKES NO AND DISCLAIMS ANY REPRESENTATION OR WARRANTY OF MERCHANTABILITY OR FITNESS FOR ANY PARTICULAR PURPOSE OR THAT THE USE OF THE SOFTWARE WILL NOT INFRINGE ANY THIRD PARTY RIGHTS.

4. BEOPEN SHALL NOT BE LIABLE TO LICENSEE OR ANY OTHER USERS OF THE SOFTWARE FOR ANY INCIDENTAL, SPECIAL, OR CONSEQUENTIAL DAMAGES OR LOSS AS A RESULT OF USING, MODIFYING OR DISTRIBUTING THE SOFTWARE, OR ANY DERIVATIVE THEREOF, EVEN IF ADVISED OF THE POSSIBILITY THEREOF.

5. This License Agreement will automatically terminate upon a material breach of its terms and conditions.

6. This License Agreement shall be governed by and interpreted in all respects by the law of the State of California, excluding conflict of law provisions. Nothing in this License Agreement shall be deemed to create any relationship of agency, partnership, or joint venture between BeOpen and Licensee. This License Agreement does not grant permission to use BeOpen trademarks or trade names in a trademark sense to endorse or promote products or services of Licensee, or any third party. As an exception, the "BeOpen Python" logos available at http://www.pythonlabs.com/logos.html may be used according to the permissions granted on that web page.

7. By copying, installing or otherwise using the software, Licensee agrees to be bound by the terms and conditions of this License Agreement.

CNRI LICENSE AGREEMENT FOR PYTHON 1.6.1

1. This LICENSE AGREEMENT is between the Corporation for National Research Initiatives, having an office at 1895 Preston White Drive, Reston, VA 20191 ("CNRI"), and the Individual or Organization ("Licensee") accessing and otherwise using Python 1.6.1 software in source or binary form and its associated documentation.

2. Subject to the terms and conditions of this License Agreement, CNRI hereby grants Licensee a nonexclusive, royalty-free, world-wide license to reproduce, analyze, test, perform and/or display publicly, prepare derivative works, distribute, and otherwise use Python 1.6.1 alone or in any derivative version, provided, however, that CNRI's License Agreement and CNRI's notice of copyright, i.e., "Copyright © 1995-2001 Corporation for National Research Initiatives; All Rights Reserved" are retained in Python 1.6.1 alone or in any derivative version prepared by Licensee. Alternately, in lieu of CNRI's License Agreement, Licensee may substitute the following text (omitting the quotes): "Python 1.6.1 is made available subject to the terms and conditions in CNRI's License Agreement. This Agreement together with Python 1.6.1 may be located on the Internet using the following unique, persistent identifier (known as a handle): 1895.22/1013. This Agreement may also be obtained from a proxy server on the Internet using the following URL: http://hdl.handle.net/1895.22/1013."

3. In the event Licensee prepares a derivative work that is based on or incorporates Python 1.6.1 or any part thereof, and wants to make the derivative work available to others as provided herein, then Licensee hereby agrees to include in any such work a brief summary of the changes made to Python 1.6.1.

4. CNRI is making Python 1.6.1 available to Licensee on an "AS IS" basis. CNRI MAKES NO REPRESENTATIONS OR WARRANTIES, EXPRESS OR IMPLIED. BY WAY OF EXAMPLE, BUT NOT LIMITATION, CNRI MAKES NO AND DISCLAIMS ANY REPRESENTATION OR WARRANTY OF MERCHANTABILITY OR FITNESS FOR ANY PARTICULAR PURPOSE OR THAT THE USE OF PYTHON 1.6.1 WILL NOT INFRINGE ANY THIRD PARTY RIGHTS.

5. CNRI SHALL NOT BE LIABLE TO LICENSEE OR ANY OTHER USERS OF PYTHON 1.6.1 FOR ANY INCIDENTAL, SPECIAL, OR CONSEQUENTIAL DAMAGES OR LOSS AS A RESULT OF MODIFYING, DISTRIBUTING, OR OTHERWISE USING PYTHON 1.6.1, OR ANY DERIVATIVE THEREOF, EVEN IF ADVISED OF THE POSSIBILITY THEREOF.

6. This License Agreement will automatically terminate upon a material breach of its terms and conditions.

7. This License Agreement shall be governed by the federal intellectual property law of the United States, including without limitation the federal copyright law, and, to the extent such U.S. federal law does not apply, by the law of the Commonwealth of Virginia, excluding Virginia's conflict of law provisions. Notwithstanding the foregoing, with regard to derivative works based on Python 1.6.1 that incorporate non-separable material that was previously distributed under the GNU General Public License (GPL), the law of the Commonwealth of Virginia shall govern this License Agreement only as to issues arising under or with respect to Paragraphs 4, 5, and 7 of this License Agreement. Nothing in this License Agreement shall be deemed to create any relationship of agency, partnership, or joint venture between CNRI and Licensee. This License Agreement does not grant permission to use CNRI trademarks or trade name in a trademark sense to endorse or promote products or services of Licensee, or any third party.

8. By clicking on the "ACCEPT" button where indicated, or by copying, installing or otherwise using Python 1.6.1, Licensee agrees to be bound by the terms and conditions of this License Agreement.

ACCEPT

CWI LICENSE AGREEMENT FOR PYTHON 0.9.0 THROUGH 1.2

Copyright © 1991 - 1995, Stichting Mathematisch Centrum Amsterdam, The Netherlands. All rights reserved.

Permission to use, copy, modify, and distribute this software and its documentation for any purpose and without fee is hereby granted, provided that the above copyright notice appear in all copies and that both that copyright notice and this permission notice appear in supporting documentation, and that the name of Stichting Mathematisch Centrum or CWI not be used in advertising or publicity pertaining to distribution of the software without specific, written prior permission.

STICHTING MATHEMATISCH CENTRUM DISCLAIMS ALL WARRANTIES WITH REGARD TO THIS SOFT-WARE, INCLUDING ALL IMPLIED WARRANTIES OF MERCHANTABILITY AND FITNESS, IN NO EVENT SHALL STICHTING MATHEMATISCH CENTRUM BE LIABLE FOR ANY SPECIAL, INDIRECT OR CON-SEQUENTIAL DAMAGES OR ANY DAMAGES WHATSOEVER RESULTING FROM LOSS OF USE, DATA OR PROFITS, WHETHER IN AN ACTION OF CONTRACT, NEGLIGENCE OR OTHER TORTIOUS ACTION, ARISING OUT OF OR IN CONNECTION WITH THE USE OR PERFORMANCE OF THIS SOFTWARE.

C.3 Licenses and Acknowledgements for Incorporated Software

This section is an incomplete, but growing list of licenses and acknowledgements for third-party software incorporated in the Python distribution.

C.3.1 Mersenne Twister

The _random module includes code based on a download from http://www.math.sci.hiroshima-u.ac.jp/~m-mat/MT/MT2002/emt19937ar.html. The following are the verbatim comments from the original code:

```
A C-program for MT19937, with initialization improved 2002/1/26.
Coded by Takuji Nishimura and Makoto Matsumoto.

Before using, initialize the state by using init_genrand(seed)
or init_by_array(init_key, key_length).

Copyright (C) 1997 - 2002, Makoto Matsumoto and Takuji Nishimura,
All rights reserved.

Redistribution and use in source and binary forms, with or without
modification, are permitted provided that the following conditions
are met:

  1. Redistributions of source code must retain the above copyright
     notice, this list of conditions and the following disclaimer.

  2. Redistributions in binary form must reproduce the above copyright
     notice, this list of conditions and the following disclaimer in the
     documentation and/or other materials provided with the distribution.

  3. The names of its contributors may not be used to endorse or promote
     products derived from this software without specific prior written
     permission.

THIS SOFTWARE IS PROVIDED BY THE COPYRIGHT HOLDERS AND CONTRIBUTORS
"AS IS" AND ANY EXPRESS OR IMPLIED WARRANTIES, INCLUDING, BUT NOT
```

```
LIMITED TO, THE IMPLIED WARRANTIES OF MERCHANTABILITY AND FITNESS FOR
A PARTICULAR PURPOSE ARE DISCLAIMED.  IN NO EVENT SHALL THE COPYRIGHT OWNER OR
CONTRIBUTORS BE LIABLE FOR ANY DIRECT, INDIRECT, INCIDENTAL, SPECIAL,
EXEMPLARY, OR CONSEQUENTIAL DAMAGES (INCLUDING, BUT NOT LIMITED TO,
PROCUREMENT OF SUBSTITUTE GOODS OR SERVICES; LOSS OF USE, DATA, OR
PROFITS; OR BUSINESS INTERRUPTION) HOWEVER CAUSED AND ON ANY THEORY OF
LIABILITY, WHETHER IN CONTRACT, STRICT LIABILITY, OR TORT (INCLUDING
NEGLIGENCE OR OTHERWISE) ARISING IN ANY WAY OUT OF THE USE OF THIS
SOFTWARE, EVEN IF ADVISED OF THE POSSIBILITY OF SUCH DAMAGE.


Any feedback is very welcome.
http://www.math.sci.hiroshima-u.ac.jp/~m-mat/MT/emt.html
email: m-mat @ math.sci.hiroshima-u.ac.jp (remove space)
```

C.3.2 Sockets

The socket module uses the functions, getaddrinfo(), and getnameinfo(), which are coded in separate source files from the WIDE Project, http://www.wide.ad.jp/.

```
Copyright (C) 1995, 1996, 1997, and 1998 WIDE Project.
All rights reserved.

Redistribution and use in source and binary forms, with or without
modification, are permitted provided that the following conditions
are met:
1. Redistributions of source code must retain the above copyright
   notice, this list of conditions and the following disclaimer.
2. Redistributions in binary form must reproduce the above copyright
   notice, this list of conditions and the following disclaimer in the
   documentation and/or other materials provided with the distribution.
3. Neither the name of the project nor the names of its contributors
   may be used to endorse or promote products derived from this software
   without specific prior written permission.

THIS SOFTWARE IS PROVIDED BY THE PROJECT AND CONTRIBUTORS ``AS IS'' AND
GAI_ANY EXPRESS OR IMPLIED WARRANTIES, INCLUDING, BUT NOT LIMITED TO, THE
IMPLIED WARRANTIES OF MERCHANTABILITY AND FITNESS FOR A PARTICULAR PURPOSE
ARE DISCLAIMED.  IN NO EVENT SHALL THE PROJECT OR CONTRIBUTORS BE LIABLE
FOR GAI_ANY DIRECT, INDIRECT, INCIDENTAL, SPECIAL, EXEMPLARY, OR CONSEQUENTIAL
DAMAGES (INCLUDING, BUT NOT LIMITED TO, PROCUREMENT OF SUBSTITUTE GOODS
OR SERVICES; LOSS OF USE, DATA, OR PROFITS; OR BUSINESS INTERRUPTION)
HOWEVER CAUSED AND ON GAI_ANY THEORY OF LIABILITY, WHETHER IN CONTRACT, STRICT
LIABILITY, OR TORT (INCLUDING NEGLIGENCE OR OTHERWISE) ARISING IN GAI_ANY WAY
OUT OF THE USE OF THIS SOFTWARE, EVEN IF ADVISED OF THE POSSIBILITY OF
SUCH DAMAGE.
```

C.3.3 Floating point exception control

The source for the fpectl module includes the following notice:

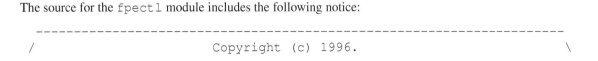

```
---------------------------------------------------------------------
   /                       Copyright (c) 1996.                       \
```

```
|            The Regents of the University of California.            |
|                      All rights reserved.                         |
|                                                                   |
|  Permission to use, copy, modify, and distribute this software for |
|  any purpose without fee is hereby granted, provided that this en- |
|  tire notice is included in all copies of any software which is or |
|  includes   a   copy   or   modification   of   this software and in all |
|  copies of the supporting documentation for such software.        |
|                                                                   |
|  This  work was produced at the University of California, Lawrence |
|  Livermore National Laboratory under   contract   no.   W-7405-ENG-48 |
|  between   the   U.S.   Department   of   Energy and The Regents of the |
|  University of California for the operation of UC LLNL.            |
|                                                                   |
|                         DISCLAIMER                                |
|                                                                   |
|  This  software was prepared as an account of work sponsored by an |
|  agency of the United States Government. Neither the United States |
|  Government  nor the University of California nor any of their em- |
|  ployees, makes any warranty, express or implied, or   assumes   any |
|  liability  or  responsibility  for the accuracy, completeness, or |
|  usefulness of any information,  apparatus,  product,  or  process |
|  disclosed,   or  represents  that  its  use  would  not  infringe |
|  privately-owned rights. Reference herein to any specific   commer- |
|  cial  products,  process,  or  service  by trade name, trademark, |
|  manufacturer, or otherwise, does not   necessarily  constitute  or |
|  imply  its endorsement, recommendation, or favoring by the United |
|  States Government or the University of California. The views   and |
|  opinions  of authors expressed herein do not necessarily state or |
|  reflect those of the United States Government or   the   University |
|  of  California,  and shall not be used for advertising or product |
\  endorsement purposes.                                            /
 -------------------------------------------------------------------
```

C.3.4 MD5 message digest algorithm

The source code for the md5 module contains the following notice:

```
Copyright (C) 1999, 2002 Aladdin Enterprises.  All rights reserved.

This software is provided 'as-is', without any express or implied
warranty.  In no event will the authors be held liable for any damages
arising from the use of this software.

Permission is granted to anyone to use this software for any purpose,
including commercial applications, and to alter it and redistribute it
freely, subject to the following restrictions:

1. The origin of this software must not be misrepresented; you must not
   claim that you wrote the original software. If you use this software
   in a product, an acknowledgment in the product documentation would be
   appreciated but is not required.
2. Altered source versions must be plainly marked as such, and must not be
   misrepresented as being the original software.
```

3. This notice may not be removed or altered from any source distribution.

L. Peter Deutsch
ghost@aladdin.com

Independent implementation of MD5 (RFC 1321).

This code implements the MD5 Algorithm defined in RFC 1321, whose
text is available at
        http://www.ietf.org/rfc/rfc1321.txt
The code is derived from the text of the RFC, including the test suite
(section A.5) but excluding the rest of Appendix A. It does not include
any code or documentation that is identified in the RFC as being
copyrighted.

The original and principal author of md5.h is L. Peter Deutsch
<ghost@aladdin.com>. Other authors are noted in the change history
that follows (in reverse chronological order):

2002-04-13 lpd Removed support for non-ANSI compilers; removed
        references to Ghostscript; clarified derivation from RFC 1321;
        now handles byte order either statically or dynamically.
1999-11-04 lpd Edited comments slightly for automatic TOC extraction.
1999-10-18 lpd Fixed typo in header comment (ansi2knr rather than md5);
        added conditionalization for C++ compilation from Martin
        Purschke <purschke@bnl.gov>.
1999-05-03 lpd Original version.

C.3.5 Asynchronous socket services

The asynchat and asyncore modules contain the following notice:

Copyright 1996 by Sam Rushing

                        All Rights Reserved

Permission to use, copy, modify, and distribute this software and
its documentation for any purpose and without fee is hereby
granted, provided that the above copyright notice appear in all
copies and that both that copyright notice and this permission
notice appear in supporting documentation, and that the name of Sam
Rushing not be used in advertising or publicity pertaining to
distribution of the software without specific, written prior
permission.

SAM RUSHING DISCLAIMS ALL WARRANTIES WITH REGARD TO THIS SOFTWARE,
INCLUDING ALL IMPLIED WARRANTIES OF MERCHANTABILITY AND FITNESS, IN
NO EVENT SHALL SAM RUSHING BE LIABLE FOR ANY SPECIAL, INDIRECT OR
CONSEQUENTIAL DAMAGES OR ANY DAMAGES WHATSOEVER RESULTING FROM LOSS
OF USE, DATA OR PROFITS, WHETHER IN AN ACTION OF CONTRACT,
NEGLIGENCE OR OTHER TORTIOUS ACTION, ARISING OUT OF OR IN
CONNECTION WITH THE USE OR PERFORMANCE OF THIS SOFTWARE.

C.3.6 Cookie management

The `Cookie` module contains the following notice:

```
Copyright 2000 by Timothy O'Malley <timo@alum.mit.edu>

                All Rights Reserved

Permission to use, copy, modify, and distribute this software
and its documentation for any purpose and without fee is hereby
granted, provided that the above copyright notice appear in all
copies and that both that copyright notice and this permission
notice appear in supporting documentation, and that the name of
Timothy O'Malley  not be used in advertising or publicity
pertaining to distribution of the software without specific, written
prior permission.

Timothy O'Malley DISCLAIMS ALL WARRANTIES WITH REGARD TO THIS
SOFTWARE, INCLUDING ALL IMPLIED WARRANTIES OF MERCHANTABILITY
AND FITNESS, IN NO EVENT SHALL Timothy O'Malley BE LIABLE FOR
ANY SPECIAL, INDIRECT OR CONSEQUENTIAL DAMAGES OR ANY DAMAGES
WHATSOEVER RESULTING FROM LOSS OF USE, DATA OR PROFITS,
WHETHER IN AN ACTION OF CONTRACT, NEGLIGENCE OR OTHER TORTIOUS
ACTION, ARISING OUT OF OR IN CONNECTION WITH THE USE OR
PERFORMANCE OF THIS SOFTWARE.
```

C.3.7 Execution tracing

The `trace` module contains the following notice:

```
portions copyright 2001, Autonomous Zones Industries, Inc., all rights...
err... reserved and offered to the public under the terms of the
Python 2.2 license.
Author: Zooko O'Whielacronx
http://zooko.com/
mailto:zooko@zooko.com

Copyright 2000, Mojam Media, Inc., all rights reserved.
Author: Skip Montanaro

Copyright 1999, Bioreason, Inc., all rights reserved.
Author: Andrew Dalke

Copyright 1995-1997, Automatrix, Inc., all rights reserved.
Author: Skip Montanaro

Copyright 1991-1995, Stichting Mathematisch Centrum, all rights reserved.


Permission to use, copy, modify, and distribute this Python software and
its associated documentation for any purpose without fee is hereby
granted, provided that the above copyright notice appears in all copies,
and that both that copyright notice and this permission notice appear in
supporting documentation, and that the name of neither Automatrix,
```

Bioreason or Mojam Media be used in advertising or publicity pertaining to
distribution of the software without specific, written prior permission.

C.3.8 UUencode and UUdecode functions

The uu module contains the following notice:

```
Copyright 1994 by Lance Ellinghouse
Cathedral City, California Republic, United States of America.
                    All Rights Reserved
Permission to use, copy, modify, and distribute this software and its
documentation for any purpose and without fee is hereby granted,
provided that the above copyright notice appear in all copies and that
both that copyright notice and this permission notice appear in
supporting documentation, and that the name of Lance Ellinghouse
not be used in advertising or publicity pertaining to distribution
of the software without specific, written prior permission.
LANCE ELLINGHOUSE DISCLAIMS ALL WARRANTIES WITH REGARD TO
THIS SOFTWARE, INCLUDING ALL IMPLIED WARRANTIES OF MERCHANTABILITY AND
FITNESS, IN NO EVENT SHALL LANCE ELLINGHOUSE CENTRUM BE LIABLE
FOR ANY SPECIAL, INDIRECT OR CONSEQUENTIAL DAMAGES OR ANY DAMAGES
WHATSOEVER RESULTING FROM LOSS OF USE, DATA OR PROFITS, WHETHER IN AN
ACTION OF CONTRACT, NEGLIGENCE OR OTHER TORTIOUS ACTION, ARISING OUT
OF OR IN CONNECTION WITH THE USE OR PERFORMANCE OF THIS SOFTWARE.


Modified by Jack Jansen, CWI, July 1995:
- Use binascii module to do the actual line-by-line conversion
  between ascii and binary. This results in a 1000-fold speedup. The C
  version is still 5 times faster, though.
- Arguments more compliant with Python standard
```

C.3.9 XML Remote Procedure Calls

The xmlrpclib module contains the following notice:

```
    The XML-RPC client interface is

Copyright (c) 1999-2002 by Secret Labs AB
Copyright (c) 1999-2002 by Fredrik Lundh

By obtaining, using, and/or copying this software and/or its
associated documentation, you agree that you have read, understood,
and will comply with the following terms and conditions:

Permission to use, copy, modify, and distribute this software and
its associated documentation for any purpose and without fee is
hereby granted, provided that the above copyright notice appears in
all copies, and that both that copyright notice and this permission
notice appear in supporting documentation, and that the name of
Secret Labs AB or the author not be used in advertising or publicity
pertaining to distribution of the software without specific, written
prior permission.
```

```
SECRET LABS AB AND THE AUTHOR DISCLAIMS ALL WARRANTIES WITH REGARD
TO THIS SOFTWARE, INCLUDING ALL IMPLIED WARRANTIES OF MERCHANT-
ABILITY AND FITNESS.  IN NO EVENT SHALL SECRET LABS AB OR THE AUTHOR
BE LIABLE FOR ANY SPECIAL, INDIRECT OR CONSEQUENTIAL DAMAGES OR ANY
DAMAGES WHATSOEVER RESULTING FROM LOSS OF USE, DATA OR PROFITS,
WHETHER IN AN ACTION OF CONTRACT, NEGLIGENCE OR OTHER TORTIOUS
ACTION, ARISING OUT OF OR IN CONNECTION WITH THE USE OR PERFORMANCE
OF THIS SOFTWARE.
```

C.3.10 test_epoll

The `test_epoll` contains the following notice:

```
Copyright (c) 2001-2006 Twisted Matrix Laboratories.

Permission is hereby granted, free of charge, to any person obtaining
a copy of this software and associated documentation files (the
"Software"), to deal in the Software without restriction, including
without limitation the rights to use, copy, modify, merge, publish,
distribute, sublicense, and/or sell copies of the Software, and to
permit persons to whom the Software is furnished to do so, subject to
the following conditions:

The above copyright notice and this permission notice shall be
included in all copies or substantial portions of the Software.

THE SOFTWARE IS PROVIDED "AS IS", WITHOUT WARRANTY OF ANY KIND,
EXPRESS OR IMPLIED, INCLUDING BUT NOT LIMITED TO THE WARRANTIES OF
MERCHANTABILITY, FITNESS FOR A PARTICULAR PURPOSE AND
NONINFRINGEMENT. IN NO EVENT SHALL THE AUTHORS OR COPYRIGHT HOLDERS BE
LIABLE FOR ANY CLAIM, DAMAGES OR OTHER LIABILITY, WHETHER IN AN ACTION
OF CONTRACT, TORT OR OTHERWISE, ARISING FROM, OUT OF OR IN CONNECTION
WITH THE SOFTWARE OR THE USE OR OTHER DEALINGS IN THE SOFTWARE.
```

C.3.11 Select kqueue

The `select` and contains the following notice for the kqueue interface:

```
Copyright (c) 2000 Doug White, 2006 James Knight, 2007 Christian Heimes
All rights reserved.

Redistribution and use in source and binary forms, with or without
modification, are permitted provided that the following conditions
are met:
1. Redistributions of source code must retain the above copyright
   notice, this list of conditions and the following disclaimer.
2. Redistributions in binary form must reproduce the above copyright
   notice, this list of conditions and the following disclaimer in the
   documentation and/or other materials provided with the distribution.

THIS SOFTWARE IS PROVIDED BY THE AUTHOR AND CONTRIBUTORS ``AS IS'' AND
ANY EXPRESS OR IMPLIED WARRANTIES, INCLUDING, BUT NOT LIMITED TO, THE
IMPLIED WARRANTIES OF MERCHANTABILITY AND FITNESS FOR A PARTICULAR PURPOSE
```

ARE DISCLAIMED. IN NO EVENT SHALL THE AUTHOR OR CONTRIBUTORS BE LIABLE
FOR ANY DIRECT, INDIRECT, INCIDENTAL, SPECIAL, EXEMPLARY, OR CONSEQUENTIAL
DAMAGES (INCLUDING, BUT NOT LIMITED TO, PROCUREMENT OF SUBSTITUTE GOODS
OR SERVICES; LOSS OF USE, DATA, OR PROFITS; OR BUSINESS INTERRUPTION)
HOWEVER CAUSED AND ON ANY THEORY OF LIABILITY, WHETHER IN CONTRACT, STRICT
LIABILITY, OR TORT (INCLUDING NEGLIGENCE OR OTHERWISE) ARISING IN ANY WAY
OUT OF THE USE OF THIS SOFTWARE, EVEN IF ADVISED OF THE POSSIBILITY OF
SUCH DAMAGE.

C.3.12 strtod and dtoa

The file `Python/dtoa.c`, which supplies C functions dtoa and strtod for conversion of C doubles to and from strings, is derived from the file of the same name by David M. Gay, currently available from http://www.netlib.org/fp/. The original file, as retrieved on March 16, 2009, contains the following copyright and licensing notice:

```
/****************************************************************
 *
 * The author of this software is David M. Gay.
 *
 * Copyright (c) 1991, 2000, 2001 by Lucent Technologies.
 *
 * Permission to use, copy, modify, and distribute this software for any
 * purpose without fee is hereby granted, provided that this entire notice
 * is included in all copies of any software which is or includes a copy
 * or modification of this software and in all copies of the supporting
 * documentation for such software.
 *
 * THIS SOFTWARE IS BEING PROVIDED "AS IS", WITHOUT ANY EXPRESS OR IMPLIED
 * WARRANTY.  IN PARTICULAR, NEITHER THE AUTHOR NOR LUCENT MAKES ANY
 * REPRESENTATION OR WARRANTY OF ANY KIND CONCERNING THE MERCHANTABILITY
 * OF THIS SOFTWARE OR ITS FITNESS FOR ANY PARTICULAR PURPOSE.
 *
 ***************************************************************/
```

C.3.13 OpenSSL

The modules `hashlib`, `posix`, `ssl`, `crypt` use the OpenSSL library for added performance if made available by the operating system. Additionally, the Windows and Mac OS X installers for Python may include a copy of the OpenSSL libraries, so we include a copy of the OpenSSL license here:

```
LICENSE ISSUES
==============

The OpenSSL toolkit stays under a dual license, i.e. both the conditions of
the OpenSSL License and the original SSLeay license apply to the toolkit.
See below for the actual license texts. Actually both licenses are BSD-style
Open Source licenses. In case of any license issues related to OpenSSL
please contact openssl-core@openssl.org.

OpenSSL License
---------------

  /* ====================================================================
```

```
* Copyright (c) 1998-2008 The OpenSSL Project.  All rights reserved.
*
* Redistribution and use in source and binary forms, with or without
* modification, are permitted provided that the following conditions
* are met:
*
* 1. Redistributions of source code must retain the above copyright
*    notice, this list of conditions and the following disclaimer.
*
* 2. Redistributions in binary form must reproduce the above copyright
*    notice, this list of conditions and the following disclaimer in
*    the documentation and/or other materials provided with the
*    distribution.
*
* 3. All advertising materials mentioning features or use of this
*    software must display the following acknowledgment:
*    "This product includes software developed by the OpenSSL Project
*    for use in the OpenSSL Toolkit. (http://www.openssl.org/)"
*
* 4. The names "OpenSSL Toolkit" and "OpenSSL Project" must not be used to
*    endorse or promote products derived from this software without
*    prior written permission. For written permission, please contact
*    openssl-core@openssl.org.
*
* 5. Products derived from this software may not be called "OpenSSL"
*    nor may "OpenSSL" appear in their names without prior written
*    permission of the OpenSSL Project.
*
* 6. Redistributions of any form whatsoever must retain the following
*    acknowledgment:
*    "This product includes software developed by the OpenSSL Project
*    for use in the OpenSSL Toolkit (http://www.openssl.org/)"
*
* THIS SOFTWARE IS PROVIDED BY THE OpenSSL PROJECT ``AS IS'' AND ANY
* EXPRESSED OR IMPLIED WARRANTIES, INCLUDING, BUT NOT LIMITED TO, THE
* IMPLIED WARRANTIES OF MERCHANTABILITY AND FITNESS FOR A PARTICULAR
* PURPOSE ARE DISCLAIMED.  IN NO EVENT SHALL THE OpenSSL PROJECT OR
* ITS CONTRIBUTORS BE LIABLE FOR ANY DIRECT, INDIRECT, INCIDENTAL,
* SPECIAL, EXEMPLARY, OR CONSEQUENTIAL DAMAGES (INCLUDING, BUT
* NOT LIMITED TO, PROCUREMENT OF SUBSTITUTE GOODS OR SERVICES;
* LOSS OF USE, DATA, OR PROFITS; OR BUSINESS INTERRUPTION)
* HOWEVER CAUSED AND ON ANY THEORY OF LIABILITY, WHETHER IN CONTRACT,
* STRICT LIABILITY, OR TORT (INCLUDING NEGLIGENCE OR OTHERWISE)
* ARISING IN ANY WAY OUT OF THE USE OF THIS SOFTWARE, EVEN IF ADVISED
* OF THE POSSIBILITY OF SUCH DAMAGE.
* ======================================================================
*
* This product includes cryptographic software written by Eric Young
* (eay@cryptsoft.com).  This product includes software written by Tim
* Hudson (tjh@cryptsoft.com).
*
*/

Original SSLeay License
```

```
----------------------

/* Copyright (C) 1995-1998 Eric Young (eay@cryptsoft.com)
 * All rights reserved.
 *
 * This package is an SSL implementation written
 * by Eric Young (eay@cryptsoft.com).
 * The implementation was written so as to conform with Netscapes SSL.
 *
 * This library is free for commercial and non-commercial use as long as
 * the following conditions are aheared to.  The following conditions
 * apply to all code found in this distribution, be it the RC4, RSA,
 * lhash, DES, etc., code; not just the SSL code.  The SSL documentation
 * included with this distribution is covered by the same copyright terms
 * except that the holder is Tim Hudson (tjh@cryptsoft.com).
 *
 * Copyright remains Eric Young's, and as such any Copyright notices in
 * the code are not to be removed.
 * If this package is used in a product, Eric Young should be given attribution
 * as the author of the parts of the library used.
 * This can be in the form of a textual message at program startup or
 * in documentation (online or textual) provided with the package.
 *
 * Redistribution and use in source and binary forms, with or without
 * modification, are permitted provided that the following conditions
 * are met:
 * 1. Redistributions of source code must retain the copyright
 *    notice, this list of conditions and the following disclaimer.
 * 2. Redistributions in binary form must reproduce the above copyright
 *    notice, this list of conditions and the following disclaimer in the
 *    documentation and/or other materials provided with the distribution.
 * 3. All advertising materials mentioning features or use of this software
 *    must display the following acknowledgement:
 *    "This product includes cryptographic software written by
 *     Eric Young (eay@cryptsoft.com)"
 *    The word 'cryptographic' can be left out if the rouines from the library
 *    being used are not cryptographic related :-).
 * 4. If you include any Windows specific code (or a derivative thereof) from
 *    the apps directory (application code) you must include an acknowledgement:
 *    "This product includes software written by Tim Hudson (tjh@cryptsoft.com)"
 *
 * THIS SOFTWARE IS PROVIDED BY ERIC YOUNG ``AS IS'' AND
 * ANY EXPRESS OR IMPLIED WARRANTIES, INCLUDING, BUT NOT LIMITED TO, THE
 * IMPLIED WARRANTIES OF MERCHANTABILITY AND FITNESS FOR A PARTICULAR PURPOSE
 * ARE DISCLAIMED.  IN NO EVENT SHALL THE AUTHOR OR CONTRIBUTORS BE LIABLE
 * FOR ANY DIRECT, INDIRECT, INCIDENTAL, SPECIAL, EXEMPLARY, OR CONSEQUENTIAL
 * DAMAGES (INCLUDING, BUT NOT LIMITED TO, PROCUREMENT OF SUBSTITUTE GOODS
 * OR SERVICES; LOSS OF USE, DATA, OR PROFITS; OR BUSINESS INTERRUPTION)
 * HOWEVER CAUSED AND ON ANY THEORY OF LIABILITY, WHETHER IN CONTRACT, STRICT
 * LIABILITY, OR TORT (INCLUDING NEGLIGENCE OR OTHERWISE) ARISING IN ANY WAY
 * OUT OF THE USE OF THIS SOFTWARE, EVEN IF ADVISED OF THE POSSIBILITY OF
 * SUCH DAMAGE.
 *
 * The licence and distribution terms for any publically available version or
```

```
* derivative of this code cannot be changed.  i.e. this code cannot simply be
* copied and put under another distribution licence
* [including the GNU Public Licence.]
*/
```

C.3.14 expat

The `pyexpat` extension is built using an included copy of the expat sources unless the build is configured `--with-system-expat`:

```
Copyright (c) 1998, 1999, 2000 Thai Open Source Software Center Ltd
                     and Clark Cooper

Permission is hereby granted, free of charge, to any person obtaining
a copy of this software and associated documentation files (the
"Software"), to deal in the Software without restriction, including
without limitation the rights to use, copy, modify, merge, publish,
distribute, sublicense, and/or sell copies of the Software, and to
permit persons to whom the Software is furnished to do so, subject to
the following conditions:

The above copyright notice and this permission notice shall be included
in all copies or substantial portions of the Software.

THE SOFTWARE IS PROVIDED "AS IS", WITHOUT WARRANTY OF ANY KIND,
EXPRESS OR IMPLIED, INCLUDING BUT NOT LIMITED TO THE WARRANTIES OF
MERCHANTABILITY, FITNESS FOR A PARTICULAR PURPOSE AND NONINFRINGEMENT.
IN NO EVENT SHALL THE AUTHORS OR COPYRIGHT HOLDERS BE LIABLE FOR ANY
CLAIM, DAMAGES OR OTHER LIABILITY, WHETHER IN AN ACTION OF CONTRACT,
TORT OR OTHERWISE, ARISING FROM, OUT OF OR IN CONNECTION WITH THE
SOFTWARE OR THE USE OR OTHER DEALINGS IN THE SOFTWARE.
```

C.3.15 libffi

The `_ctypes` extension is built using an included copy of the libffi sources unless the build is configured `--with-system-libffi`:

```
Copyright (c) 1996-2008  Red Hat, Inc and others.

Permission is hereby granted, free of charge, to any person obtaining
a copy of this software and associated documentation files (the
``Software''), to deal in the Software without restriction, including
without limitation the rights to use, copy, modify, merge, publish,
distribute, sublicense, and/or sell copies of the Software, and to
permit persons to whom the Software is furnished to do so, subject to
the following conditions:

The above copyright notice and this permission notice shall be included
in all copies or substantial portions of the Software.

THE SOFTWARE IS PROVIDED ``AS IS'', WITHOUT WARRANTY OF ANY KIND,
EXPRESS OR IMPLIED, INCLUDING BUT NOT LIMITED TO THE WARRANTIES OF
MERCHANTABILITY, FITNESS FOR A PARTICULAR PURPOSE AND
```

NONINFRINGEMENT. IN NO EVENT SHALL THE AUTHORS OR COPYRIGHT
HOLDERS BE LIABLE FOR ANY CLAIM, DAMAGES OR OTHER LIABILITY,
WHETHER IN AN ACTION OF CONTRACT, TORT OR OTHERWISE, ARISING FROM,
OUT OF OR IN CONNECTION WITH THE SOFTWARE OR THE USE OR OTHER
DEALINGS IN THE SOFTWARE.

C.3.16 zlib

The `zlib` extension is built using an included copy of the zlib sources if the zlib version found on the system is too old to be used for the build:

```
Copyright (C) 1995-2010 Jean-loup Gailly and Mark Adler

This software is provided 'as-is', without any express or implied
warranty.  In no event will the authors be held liable for any damages
arising from the use of this software.

Permission is granted to anyone to use this software for any purpose,
including commercial applications, and to alter it and redistribute it
freely, subject to the following restrictions:

1. The origin of this software must not be misrepresented; you must not
   claim that you wrote the original software. If you use this software
   in a product, an acknowledgment in the product documentation would be
   appreciated but is not required.

2. Altered source versions must be plainly marked as such, and must not be
   misrepresented as being the original software.

3. This notice may not be removed or altered from any source distribution.

Jean-loup Gailly        Mark Adler
jloup@gzip.org          madler@alumni.caltech.edu
```

Appendix C. History and License

COPYRIGHT

Python and this documentation is:

Copyright © 2001-2015 Python Software Foundation. All rights reserved.

Copyright © 2000 BeOpen.com. All rights reserved.

Copyright © 1995-2000 Corporation for National Research Initiatives. All rights reserved.

Copyright © 1991-1995 Stichting Mathematisch Centrum. All rights reserved.

See *History and License* for complete license and permissions information.

Symbols

*

    in function calls, 53

    statement, 78

**

    in function calls, 53

    statement, 78

**=

    augmented assignment, 63

*=

    augmented assignment, 63

+=

    augmented assignment, 63

-=

    augmented assignment, 63

..., **87**

//=

    augmented assignment, 63

/=

    augmented assignment, 63

=

    assignment statement, 61

%=

    augmented assignment, 63

&=

    augmented assignment, 63

__abs__() (object method), 36

__add__() (object method), 34

__all__ (optional module attribute), 69

__and__() (object method), 34

__bases__ (class attribute), 21

__builtin__

    module, 71, 81

__builtins__, 71

__call__() (object method), 31, 54

__class__ (instance attribute), 22

__closure__ (function attribute), 19

__cmp__() (object method), 26

__code__ (function attribute), 19

__coerce__() (object method), 36

__complex__() (object method), 36

__contains__() (object method), 33

__debug__, 64

__defaults__ (function attribute), 19

__del__() (object method), 25

__delattr__() (object method), 28

__delete__() (object method), 28

__delitem__() (object method), 32

__delslice__() (object method), 33

__dict__ (class attribute), 21

__dict__ (function attribute), 19

__dict__ (instance attribute), 22, 28

__dict__ (module attribute), 21

__div__() (object method), 35

__divmod__() (object method), 34

__doc__ (class attribute), 21

__doc__ (function attribute), 19

__doc__ (method attribute), 19

__doc__ (module attribute), 21

__enter__() (object method), 37

__eq__() (object method), 26

__exit__() (object method), 37

__file__, 68

__file__ (module attribute), 21

__float__() (object method), 36

__floordiv__() (object method), 34

__future__, **90**

__ge__() (object method), 26

__get__() (object method), 28

__getattr__() (object method), 27

__getattribute__() (object method), 28

__getitem__() (mapping object method), 24

__getitem__() (object method), 32

__getslice__() (object method), 33

__globals__ (function attribute), 19

__gt__() (object method), 26

__hash__() (object method), 27

__hex__() (object method), 36

__iadd__() (object method), 35

__iand__() (object method), 35

__idiv__() (object method), 35

__ifloordiv__() (object method), 35

__ilshift__() (object method), 35

__imod__() (object method), 35

__imul__() (object method), 35
__index__() (object method), 36
__init__() (object method), 20, 25
__instancecheck__() (class method), 31
__int__() (object method), 36
__invert__() (object method), 36
__ior__() (object method), 35
__ipow__() (object method), 35
__irshift__() (object method), 35
__isub__() (object method), 35
__iter__() (object method), 32
__itruediv__() (object method), 35
__ixor__() (object method), 35
__le__() (object method), 26
__len__() (mapping object method), 27
__len__() (object method), 32
__loader__, 68
__long__() (object method), 36
__lshift__() (object method), 34
__lt__() (object method), 26
__main__
      module, 42, 81
__metaclass__ (built-in variable), 30
__missing__() (object method), 32
__mod__() (object method), 34
__module__ (class attribute), 21
__module__ (function attribute), 19
__module__ (method attribute), 19
__mul__() (object method), 34
__name__, 68
__name__ (class attribute), 21
__name__ (function attribute), 19
__name__ (method attribute), 19
__name__ (module attribute), 21
__ne__() (object method), 26
__neg__() (object method), 36
__new__() (object method), 24
__nonzero__() (object method), 27, 32
__oct__() (object method), 36
__or__() (object method), 34
__package__, 68
__path__, 68
__pos__() (object method), 36
__pow__() (object method), 34
__radd__() (object method), 35
__rand__() (object method), 35
__rcmp__() (object method), 26
__rdiv__() (object method), 35
__rdivmod__() (object method), 35
__repr__() (object method), 25
__reversed__() (object method), 33
__rfloordiv__() (object method), 35
__rlshift__() (object method), 35
__rmod__() (object method), 35

__rmul__() (object method), 35
__ror__() (object method), 35
__rpow__() (object method), 35
__rrshift__() (object method), 35
__rshift__() (object method), 34
__rsub__() (object method), 35
__rtruediv__() (object method), 35
__rxor__() (object method), 35
__set__() (object method), 28
__setattr__() (object method), 27
__setitem__() (object method), 32
__setslice__() (object method), 33
__slots__, **94**
__slots__ (built-in variable), 29
__str__() (object method), 26
__sub__() (object method), 34
__subclasscheck__() (class method), 31
__truediv__() (object method), 35
__unicode__() (object method), 27
__xor__() (object method), 34
^=
      augmented assignment, 63
|=
      augmented assignment, 63
>>>, **87**
>>=
      augmented assignment, 63
<<=
      augmented assignment, 63
2to3, **87**

A
abs
      built-in function, 36
abstract base class, **87**
addition, 55
and
      bitwise, 56
      operator, 58
anonymous
      function, 58
argument, **87**
      call semantics, 52
      function, 18
      function definition, 78
arithmetic
      conversion, 45
      operation, binary, 54
      operation, unary, 54
array
      module, 18
as
      import statement, 67
      with statement, 76

ASCII, 4, 9, 10, 13, 17
assert
    statement, 64
AssertionError
    exception, 64
assertions
    debugging, 64
assignment
    attribute, 61, 62
    augmented, 63
    class attribute, 21
    class instance attribute, 22
    slicing, 63
    statement, 18, 61
    subscription, 63
    target list, 62
atom, 45
attribute, 16, **87**
    assignment, 61, 62
    assignment, class, 21
    assignment, class instance, 22
    class, 21
    class instance, 21
    deletion, 65
    generic special, 16
    reference, 51
    special, 16
AttributeError
    exception, 51
augmented
    assignment, 63

B

back-quotes, 26, 48
backslash character, 6
backward
    quotes, 26, 48
BDFL, **87**
binary
    arithmetic operation, 54
    bitwise operation, 56
binary literal, 11
binding
    global name, 70
    name, 41, 61, 67, 69, 77, 79
bitwise
    and, 56
    operation, binary, 56
    operation, unary, 54
    or, 56
    xor, 56
blank line, 7
block, 41
    code, 41

BNF, 4, 45
Boolean
    object, 16
    operation, 58
break
    statement, 67, 74, 76
bsddb
    module, 18
built-in
    method, 20
built-in function
    abs, 36
    call, 53
    chr, 17
    cmp, 26
    compile, 71
    complex, 36
    divmod, 34, 35
    eval, 71, 82
    execfile, 71
    float, 36
    globals, 71
    hash, 27
    hex, 36
    id, 15
    input, 82
    int, 36
    len, 17, 18, 32
    locals, 71
    long, 36
    object, 20, 53
    oct, 36
    open, 22
    ord, 17
    pow, 34, 35
    range, 74
    raw_input, 82
    repr, 26, 49, 61
    slice, 23
    str, 26, 49
    type, 15
    unichr, 17
    unicode, 17, 27
built-in method
    call, 53
    object, 20, 53
byte, 17
bytearray, 18
bytecode, 22, **88**
bytes-like object, **88**

C

C, 10
    language, 16, 17, 20, 56

call, 52
    built-in function, 53
    built-in method, 53
    class instance, 53
    class object, 20, 21, 53
    function, 18, 53
    instance, 31, 54
    method, 53
    procedure, 61
    user-defined function, 53
callable
    object, 18, 52
chaining
    comparisons, 56
character, 17, 51
character set, 17
chr
    built-in function, 17
class, **88**
    attribute, 21
    attribute assignment, 21
    classic, 24
    constructor, 25
    definition, 65, 79
    instance, 21
    name, 79
    new-style, 24
    object, 20, 21, 53, 79
    old-style, 24
    statement, 79
class instance
    attribute, 21
    attribute assignment, 22
    call, 53
    object, 20, 21, 53
class object
    call, 20, 21, 53
classic class, **88**
clause, 73
close() (generator method), 50
cmp
    built-in function, 26
co_argcount (code object attribute), 22
co_cellvars (code object attribute), 22
co_code (code object attribute), 22
co_consts (code object attribute), 22
co_filename (code object attribute), 22
co_firstlineno (code object attribute), 22
co_flags (code object attribute), 22
co_freevars (code object attribute), 22
co_lnotab (code object attribute), 22
co_name (code object attribute), 22
co_names (code object attribute), 22
co_nlocals (code object attribute), 22

co_stacksize (code object attribute), 22
co_varnames (code object attribute), 22
code
    block, 41
    object, 22
coercion, **88**
comma, 46
    trailing, 59, 65
command line, 81
comment, 6
comparison, 56
    string, 17
comparisons, 26
    chaining, 56
compile
    built-in function, 71
complex
    built-in function, 36
    literal, 11
    number, 17
    object, 17
complex number, **88**
compound
    statement, 73
comprehensions
    list, 46, 47
Conditional
    expression, 58
conditional
    expression, 58
constant, 9
constructor
    class, 25
container, 15, 21
context manager, 37, **88**
continue
    statement, 67, 74, 76
conversion
    arithmetic, 45
    string, 26, 48, 61
coroutine, 49
CPython, **88**

D

dangling
    else, 73
data, 15
    type, 16
    type, immutable, 46
datum, 48
dbm
    module, 18
debugging
    assertions, 64

decimal literal, 11
decorator, **88**
DEDENT token, 7, 73
def
    statement, 77
default
    parameter value, 78
definition
    class, 65, 79
    function, 65, 77
del
    statement, 25, 64
deletion
    attribute, 65
    target, 64
    target list, 64
delimiters, 13
descriptor, **89**
destructor, 25, 62
dictionary, **89**
    display, 48
    object, 18, 21, 27, 48, 51, 63
dictionary view, **89**
display
    dictionary, 48
    list, 46
    set, 48
    tuple, 46
division, 55
divmod
    built-in function, 34, 35
docstring, 79, **89**
documentation string, 22
duck-typing, **89**

E

EAFP, **89**
EBCDIC, 17
elif
    keyword, 74
Ellipsis
    object, 16
else
    dangling, 73
    keyword, 67, 74, 76
empty
    list, 47
    tuple, 17, 46
encoding declarations (source file), 6
environment, 41
error handling, 43
errors, 43
escape sequence, 10
eval

built-in function, 71, 82
evaluation
    order, 59
exc_info (in module sys), 23
exc_traceback (in module sys), 23, 75
exc_type (in module sys), 75
exc_value (in module sys), 75
except
    keyword, 75
exception, 43, 66
    AssertionError, 64
    AttributeError, 51
    GeneratorExit, 50
    handler, 23
    ImportError, 68, 69
    NameError, 46
    raising, 66
    RuntimeError, 65
    StopIteration, 49, 66
    TypeError, 54
    ValueError, 55
    ZeroDivisionError, 55
exception handler, 43
exclusive
    or, 56
exec
    statement, 71
execfile
    built-in function, 71
execution
    frame, 41, 79
    restricted, 42
    stack, 23
execution model, 41
expression, 45, **89**
    Conditional, 58
    conditional, 58
    generator, 47
    lambda, 58, 78
    list, 59, 61, 62
    statement, 61
    yield, 49
extended
    slicing, 51
extended print statement, 65
extended slicing, 17
extension
    module, 16
extension module, **89**

F

f_back (frame attribute), 22
f_builtins (frame attribute), 22
f_code (frame attribute), 22

f_exc_traceback (frame attribute), 23
f_exc_type (frame attribute), 23
f_exc_value (frame attribute), 23
f_globals (frame attribute), 22
f_lasti (frame attribute), 22
f_lineno (frame attribute), 23
f_locals (frame attribute), 22
f_restricted (frame attribute), 22
f_trace (frame attribute), 23
False, 16
file
    object, 22, 82
file object, **89**
file-like object, **89**
finally
    keyword, 65, 67, 75, 76
find_module
    finder, 68
finder, 68, **89**
    find_module, 68
float
    built-in function, 36
floating point
    number, 17
    object, 17
floating point literal, 11
floor division, **89**
for
    statement, 67, 74
frame
    execution, 41, 79
    object, 22
free
    variable, 41, 65
from
    keyword, 67
    statement, 41
frozenset
    object, 18
func_closure (function attribute), 19
func_code (function attribute), 19
func_defaults (function attribute), 19
func_dict (function attribute), 19
func_doc (function attribute), 19
func_globals (function attribute), 19
func_name (function attribute), 19
function, **89**
    anonymous, 58
    argument, 18
    call, 18, 53
    call, user-defined, 53
    definition, 65, 77
    generator, 49, 66
    name, 77

    object, 18, 20, 53, 77
    user-defined, 18
future
    statement, 69

G

garbage collection, 15, **90**
gdbm
    module, 18
generator, **90**, 90
    expression, 47
    function, 20, 49, 66
    iterator, 20, 66
    object, 22, 47, 49
generator expression, **90**, 90
GeneratorExit
    exception, 50
generic
    special attribute, 16
GIL, **90**
global
    name binding, 70
    namespace, 19
    statement, 62, 65, 70
global interpreter lock, **90**
globals
    built-in function, 71
grammar, 4
grouping, 7

H

handle an exception, 43
handler
    exception, 23
hash
    built-in function, 27
hash character, 6
hashable, 48, **90**
hex
    built-in function, 36
hexadecimal literal, 11
hierarchy
    type, 16

I

id
    built-in function, 15
identifier, 8, 46
identity
    test, 57
identity of an object, 15
IDLE, **90**
if
    statement, 74

im_class (method attribute), 19, 20
im_func (method attribute), 19, 20
im_self (method attribute), 19, 20
imaginary literal, 11
immutable, **91**
    data type, 46
    object, 17, 46, 48
immutable object, 15
immutable sequence
    object, 17
immutable types
    subclassing, 24
import
    statement, 21, 67
importer, **91**
ImportError
    exception, 68, 69
importing, **91**
in
    keyword, 74
    operator, 57
inclusive
    or, 56
INDENT token, 7
indentation, 7
index operation, 17
indices() (slice method), 23
inheritance, 79
input, 82
    built-in function, 82
    raw, 82
instance
    call, 31, 54
    class, 21
    object, 20, 21, 53
int
    built-in function, 36
integer, 17
    object, 16
    representation, 17
integer division, **91**
integer literal, 11
interactive, **91**
interactive mode, 81
internal type, 22
interpreted, **91**
interpreter, 81
inversion, 54
invocation, 18
is
    operator, 57
is not
    operator, 57
item

    sequence, 51
    string, 51
item selection, 17
iterable, **91**
iterator, **91**

J

Java
    language, 17

K

key, 48
key function, **91**
key/datum pair, 48
keyword, 8
    elif, 74
    else, 67, 74, 76
    except, 75
    finally, 65, 67, 75, 76
    from, 67
    in, 74
    yield, 49
keyword argument, **91**

L

lambda, **92**
    expression, 58, 78
language
    C, 16, 17, 20, 56
    Java, 17
    Pascal, 74
last_traceback (in module sys), 23
LBYL, **92**
leading whitespace, 7
len
    built-in function, 17, 18, 32
lexical analysis, 5
lexical definitions, 4
line continuation, 6
line joining, 5, 6
line structure, 5
list, **92**
    assignment, target, 62
    comprehensions, 46, 47
    deletion target, 64
    display, 46
    empty, 47
    expression, 59, 61, 62
    object, 18, 47, 51, 63
    target, 62, 74
list comprehension, **92**
literal, 9, 46
load_module
    loader, 68

loader, 68, **92**
    load_module, 68
locals
    built-in function, 71
logical line, 5
long
    built-in function, 36
long integer
    object, 16
long integer literal, 11
loop
    over mutable sequence, 75
    statement, 67, 74
loop control
    target, 67

M

makefile() (socket method), 22
mangling
    name, 46
mapping, **92**
    object, 18, 22, 51, 63
membership
    test, 57
metaclass, **92**
method, **92**
    built-in, 20
    call, 53
    object, 19, 20, 53
    user-defined, 19
method resolution order, **92**
minus, 54
module, **92**
    __builtin__, 71, 81
    __main__, 42, 81
    array, 18
    bsddb, 18
    dbm, 18
    extension, 16
    gdbm, 18
    importing, 67
    namespace, 21
    object, 21, 51
    sys, 65, 75, 81
modulo, 55
MRO, **92**
multiplication, 55
mutable, **92**
    object, 18, 61, 63
mutable object, 15
mutable sequence
    loop over, 75
    object, 18

N

name, 8, 41, 46
    binding, 41, 61, 67, 69, 77, 79
    binding, global, 70
    class, 79
    function, 77
    mangling, 46
    rebinding, 61
    unbinding, 65
named tuple, **92**
NameError
    exception, 46
NameError (built-in exception), 41
names
    private, 46
namespace, 41, **92**
    global, 19
    module, 21
negation, 54
nested scope, **93**
new-style class, **93**
newline
    suppression, 65
NEWLINE token, 5, 73
next() (generator method), 49
None
    object, 16, 61
not
    operator, 58
not in
    operator, 57
notation, 4
NotImplemented
    object, 16
null
    operation, 64
number, 11
    complex, 17
    floating point, 17
numeric
    object, 16, 22
numeric literal, 11

O

object, 15, **93**
    Boolean, 16
    built-in function, 20, 53
    built-in method, 20, 53
    callable, 18, 52
    class, 20, 21, 53, 79
    class instance, 20, 21, 53
    code, 22
    complex, 17
    dictionary, 18, 21, 27, 48, 51, 63

Ellipsis, 16
file, 22, 82
floating point, 17
frame, 22
frozenset, 18
function, 18, 20, 53, 77
generator, 22, 47, 49
immutable, 17, 46, 48
immutable sequence, 17
instance, 20, 21, 53
integer, 16
list, 18, 47, 51, 63
long integer, 16
mapping, 18, 22, 51, 63
method, 19, 20, 53
module, 21, 51
mutable, 18, 61, 63
mutable sequence, 18
None, 16, 61
NotImplemented, 16
numeric, 16, 22
plain integer, 16
recursive, 49
sequence, 17, 22, 51, 57, 63, 74
set, 18, 48
set type, 18
slice, 32
string, 17, 51
traceback, 23, 67, 75
tuple, 17, 51, 59
unicode, 17
user-defined function, 18, 53, 77
user-defined method, 19
oct
    built-in function, 36
octal literal, 11
open
    built-in function, 22
operation
    binary arithmetic, 54
    binary bitwise, 56
    Boolean, 58
    null, 64
    shifting, 55
    unary arithmetic, 54
    unary bitwise, 54
operator
    and, 58
    in, 57
    is, 57
    is not, 57
    not, 58
    not in, 57
    or, 58

overloading, 24
    precedence, 59
    ternary, 58
operators, 12
or
    bitwise, 56
    exclusive, 56
    inclusive, 56
    operator, 58
ord
    built-in function, 17
order
    evaluation, 59
output, 61, 65
    standard, 61, 65
OverflowError (built-in exception), 16
overloading
    operator, 24

P
package, 68, **93**
parameter, **93**
    call semantics, 52
    function definition, 77
    value, default, 78
parenthesized form, 46
parser, 5
Pascal
    language, 74
pass
    statement, 64
physical line, 5, 6, 10
plain integer
    object, 16
plain integer literal, 11
plus, 54
popen() (in module os), 22
positional argument, **93**
pow
    built-in function, 34, 35
precedence
    operator, 59
primary, 50
print
    statement, 26, 65
private
    names, 46
procedure
    call, 61
program, 81
Python 3000, **93**
Python Enhancement Proposals
    PEP 0255, 66
    PEP 0342, 50, 66

PEP 0343, 38, 77
PEP 236, 70
PEP 238, 89
PEP 278, 94
PEP 302, 68, 89, 92
PEP 308, 58
PEP 3116, 94
PEP 3119, 31
PEP 328, 69
PEP 343, 88
Pythonic, **93**

Q

quotes
    backward, 26, 48
    reverse, 26, 48

R

raise
    statement, 66
raise an exception, 43
raising
    exception, 66
range
    built-in function, 74
raw input, 82
raw string, 9
raw_input
    built-in function, 82
readline() (file method), 82
rebinding
    name, 61
recursive
    object, 49
reference
    attribute, 51
reference count, **94**
reference counting, 15
relative
    import, 69
repr
    built-in function, 26, 49, 61
representation
    integer, 17
reserved word, 8
restricted
    execution, 42
return
    statement, 65, 76
reverse
    quotes, 26, 48
RuntimeError
    exception, 65

S

scope, 41
send() (generator method), 49
sequence, **94**
    item, 51
    object, 17, 22, 51, 57, 63, 74
set
    display, 48
    object, 18, 48
set type
    object, 18
shifting
    operation, 55
simple
    statement, 61
singleton
    tuple, 17
slice, 51, **94**
    built-in function, 23
    object, 32
slicing, 17, 18, 51
    assignment, 63
    extended, 51
source character set, 6
space, 7
special
    attribute, 16
    attribute, generic, 16
special method, **94**
stack
    execution, 23
    trace, 23
standard
    output, 61, 65
Standard C, 10
standard input, 81
start (slice object attribute), 23, 52
statement, 78, **94**
    *, 78
    **, 78
    assert, 64
    assignment, 18, 61
    assignment, augmented, 63
    break, 67, 74, 76
    class, 79
    compound, 73
    continue, 67, 74, 76
    def, 77
    del, 25, 64
    exec, 71
    expression, 61
    for, 67, 74
    from, 41
    future, 69

global, 62, 65, 70
if, 74
import, 21, 67
loop, 67, 74
pass, 64
print, 26, 65
raise, 66
return, 65, 76
simple, 61
try, 23, 75
while, 67, 74
with, 37, 76
yield, 66
statement grouping, 7
stderr (in module sys), 22
stdin (in module sys), 22
stdio, 22
stdout (in module sys), 22, 65
step (slice object attribute), 23, 52
stop (slice object attribute), 23, 52
StopIteration
    exception, 49, 66
str
    built-in function, 26, 49
string
    comparison, 17
    conversion, 26, 48, 61
    item, 51
    object, 17, 51
    Unicode, 9
string literal, 9
struct sequence, **94**
subclassing
    immutable types, 24
subscription, 17, 18, 51
    assignment, 63
subtraction, 55
suite, 73
suppression
    newline, 65
syntax, 4, 45
sys
    module, 65, 75, 81
sys.exc_info, 23
sys.exc_traceback, 23
sys.last_traceback, 23
sys.meta_path, 68
sys.modules, 68
sys.path, 68
sys.path_hooks, 68
sys.path_importer_cache, 68
sys.stderr, 22
sys.stdin, 22
sys.stdout, 22

SystemExit (built-in exception), 43

T

tab, 7
target, 62
    deletion, 64
    list, 62, 74
    list assignment, 62
    list, deletion, 64
    loop control, 67
tb_frame (traceback attribute), 23
tb_lasti (traceback attribute), 23
tb_lineno (traceback attribute), 23
tb_next (traceback attribute), 23
termination model, 43
ternary
    operator, 58
test
    identity, 57
    membership, 57
throw() (generator method), 50
token, 5
trace
    stack, 23
traceback
    object, 23, 67, 75
trailing
    comma, 59, 65
triple-quoted string, 9, **94**
True, 16
try
    statement, 23, 75
tuple
    display, 46
    empty, 17, 46
    object, 17, 51, 59
    singleton, 17
type, 16, **94**
    built-in function, 15
    data, 16
    hierarchy, 16
    immutable data, 46
type of an object, 15
TypeError
    exception, 54
types, internal, 22

U

unary
    arithmetic operation, 54
    bitwise operation, 54
unbinding
    name, 65
UnboundLocalError, 41

unichr
    built-in function, 17
Unicode, 17
unicode
    built-in function, 17, 27
    object, 17
Unicode Consortium, 9
universal newlines, **94**
UNIX, 81
unreachable object, 15
unrecognized escape sequence, 10
user-defined
    function, 18
    function call, 53
    method, 19
user-defined function
    object, 18, 53, 77
user-defined method
    object, 19

V

value
    default parameter, 78
value of an object, 15
ValueError
    exception, 55
values
    writing, 61, 65
variable
    free, 41, 65
virtual environment, **94**
virtual machine, **94**

W

while
    statement, 67, 74
whitespace, 7
with
    statement, 37, 76
writing
    values, 61, 65

X

xor
    bitwise, 56

Y

yield
    expression, 49
    keyword, 49
    statement, 66

Z

Zen of Python, **94**

ZeroDivisionError
    exception, 55

www.ingramcontent.com/pod-product-compliance
Lightning Source LLC
LaVergne TN
LVHW060144070326
832902LV00018B/2937